THE
Three-Colour
DRAWING
BOOK

THE *Three-Colour* DRAWING BOOK

An Hachette UK Company
www.hachette.co.uk

First published in the United Kingdom in 2016 by
ILEX, a division of Octopus Publishing Group Ltd

Octopus Publishing Group
Carmelite House
50 Victoria Embankment
London, EC4Y 0DZ
www.octopusbooks.co.uk

Publisher: Roly Allen
Commissioning Editor: Zara Larcombe
Editor: Rachel Silverlight
Managing Specialist Editor: Frank Gallaugher
Senior Project Editor: Natalia Price-Cabrera
Art Director: Julie Weir
Designer: Anders Hanson
Picture Research Manager: Giulia Hetherington
Production Controller: Sarah Kramer

ISBN 978-1-78157-321-1

A CIP catalogue record for this book is available
from the British Library

Printed and bound in China

10 9 8 7 6 5 4 3 2

Sarah **SKEATE**

The *Three-Colour* DRAWING BOOK

DRAW
ANYTHING
IN
Red, Black & Blue
BALLPOINT!

ilex

Introduction

It's time to go old school! Find your fluffy pencil case and pull out your ballpoint pen. This book will show you how to create fabulous art using the simple ballpoint pen, with only three colors: red, blue, and black.

Ballpoints are readily available and economical to use— I've used one pen of each color for this entire book and they are still going! The only other thing you will need is plain paper. You can supplement your materials with white gouache paint, mounting board frames, stencils, and old printed books and postcards (only to be drawn on with the permission of the owner!!).

Many of the drawings in this book are broken down into steps.
These steps show the order in which the marks are made.
Drawing in a particular order:

1) Gives you the confidence to know where to begin.

2) Provides you with markers while the drawing is developing,
   which show where to position the next part of the drawing.

There are helpful drawing tips throughout the book, but to
see the most important advice all in one place, go to pages
104-105. You might want to peruse those pages before you
embark on your drawing mission.

Good luck, and most of all, enjoy yourself. Put that pencil and
eraser down ... *The ballpoint pen is your friend!*

BASIC LINES

The **very first thing** we do when we put pen to paper is draw a line. How you draw this line will affect the look of the drawing in many ways. There's no right or wrong, only what looks good to you. Many of the drawings in this book are done with a smooth line of even pressure.

If you are drawing a object that curves around and you want to keep the outline smooth and neat, rotate the page as you draw so that your pen, hand, and wrist are at the most comfortable angle.

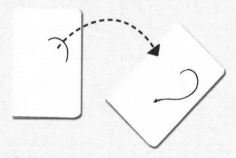

I like to add a little impact to my drawings by thickening the line in a "drop shadow" style, as below. Often used in graffiti, the drop shadow lends itself well to the ballpoint pen.

 **Tip** If you put several pages of blank paper under what you are drawing on, the ink will flow more freely, and as a result the line you draw will be thicker and more even.

BASIC SHADING

For a more detailed look at shading and textures, see pages 34–37, but here are some basic examples with ways you can use them, to get you started...

BLOCK COLOR:
Useful for the surfaces of smooth, solid objects. add highlights to further emphasize smoothness.

PARALLEL LINES:
Implies objects that are solid and static. Also good for conveying direction.

Contour lines

CROSS-HATCHING:
Good for adding form and texture—for example to fabric or natural objects.

STIPPLING (DOTS):
Gives a smooth but subtly textured finish to objects. It takes time though!

 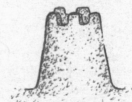 

SCRIBBLE-SHADING:
Adds form, movement, and texture to organic matter.

CREATE *Cute*

Want to create that cute look? Here's the *science* bit:

Due to evolution, babies have traits that we instinctively find cute...

- **LARGE HEAD IN RELATION TO BODY SIZE**
- **LARGE FOREHEAD (FACIAL FEATURES POSITIONED BELOW MIDWAY ON FACE)**
- **BIG ROUND EYES, WIDE APART**
- **ROUNDED CHEEKS**
- **NOSE AND MOUTH CLOSE OR LEVEL WITH EYES**

Use these proportions to create *adorable* characters!

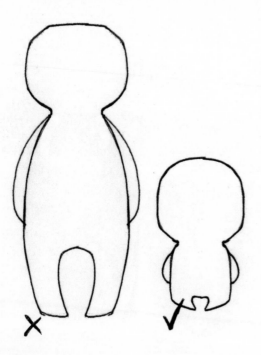

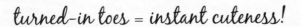

turned-in toes = instant cuteness!

You can create cute characters using simple shapes—you only need one shape that suggests head, body, and legs. Then add basic features.

HERE ARE SOME SIMPLE EXAMPLES FOR INSPIRATION

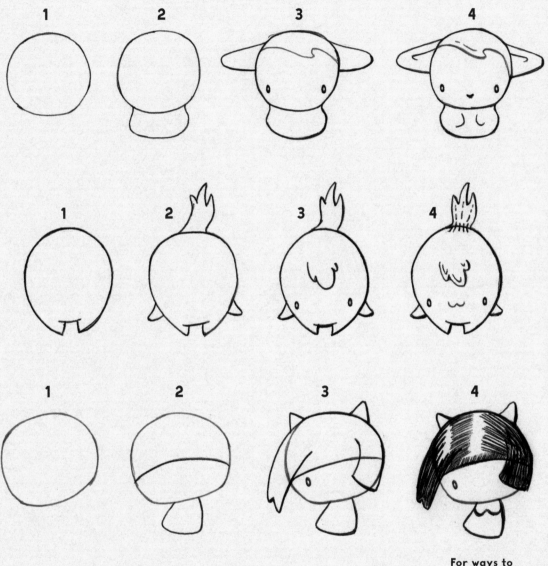

For ways to
draw hair, see
pages 44–47.

 **Tip** A good technique for ensuring that facial features fit the cute formula is to draw the eyes first and use them as a landmark to position your nose and/or mouth. This also helps you to keep the face symmetrical.

CREATE *Cute* ANIMALS

Look at pictures of animals for reference. Make the main part of the body a very simple shape. Detail should focus on the features that define the animal.

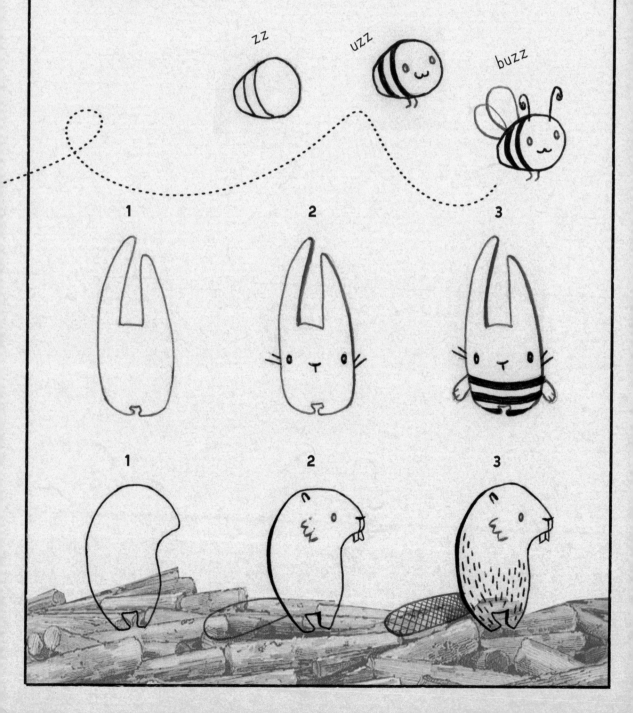

Tip

You can draw on old pictures, postcards, or textbooks (with permission!) by whitening out the background with gouache paint, then drawing over the top.

1   2   3   4

1   2   3   4

CREEPY + Cute

However spooky/creepy you wish to make your characters, you can still keep the cuteness by keeping to the proportions described on page 10. Remember keep the initial body shape simple, then add features to your liking.

The perfect combination to leave the onlooker with a feeling of unease!

Making the outline heavy can add intensity to the character.

WAYS TO CREATE CREEPY:

- BLOOD SPLATTERS
- BLANK EXPRESSIONS
- SMIRKING EXPRESSIONS

- PAIRING AN IMAGINARY CREATURE WITH ANIMAL BODY PARTS
- ADDING CLAWS AND SHARP TEETH
- ADDING SHADOWS

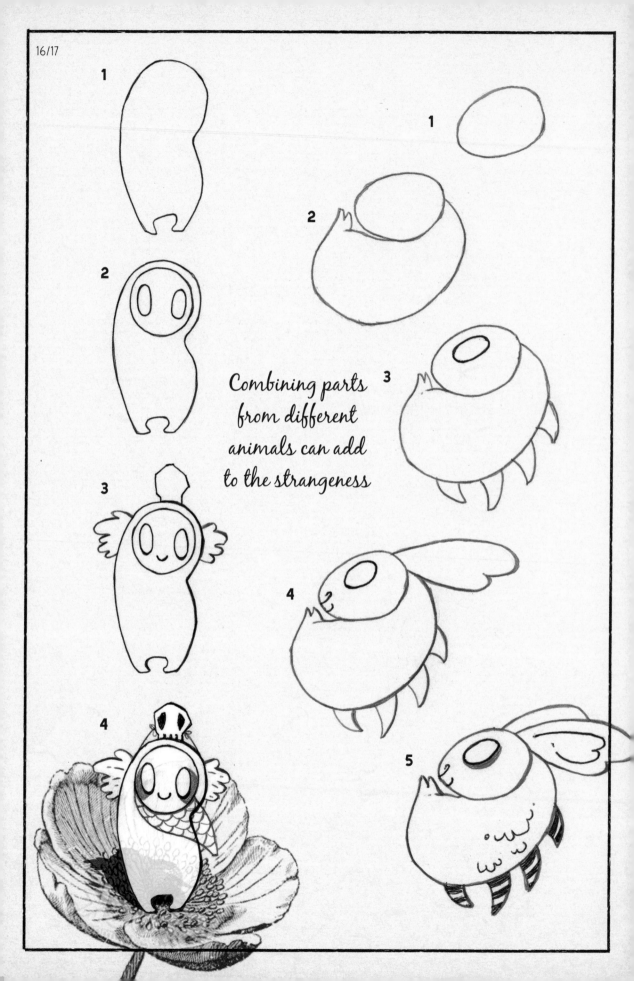

Combining parts from different animals can add to the strangeness

SOME SCARY EYES!

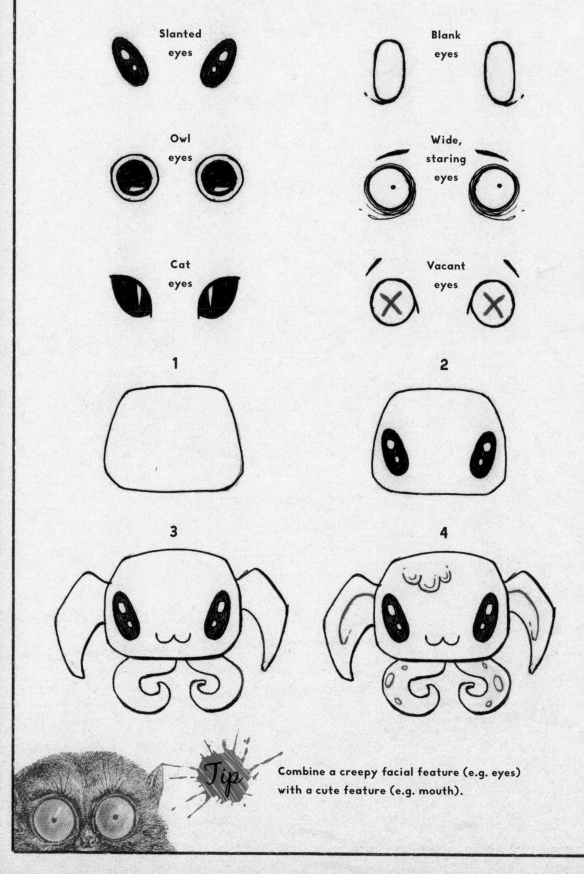

Slanted eyes

Blank eyes

Owl eyes

Wide, staring eyes

Cat eyes

Vacant eyes

1

2

3

4

Tip Combine a creepy facial feature (e.g. eyes) with a cute feature (e.g. mouth).

Start with a STENCIL

Staring down at a blank page can feel daunting. Using a shape template can help give you the confidence to put pen to paper...

Draw crescent shapes by drawing a full circle. Then move the stencil upward and re-draw part of the circle until you reach the sides of the original circle shape.

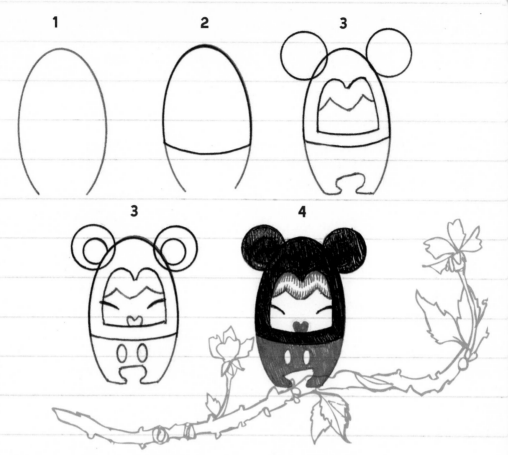

1   2   3

3   4

Use oval stencils too—good for creating cute...

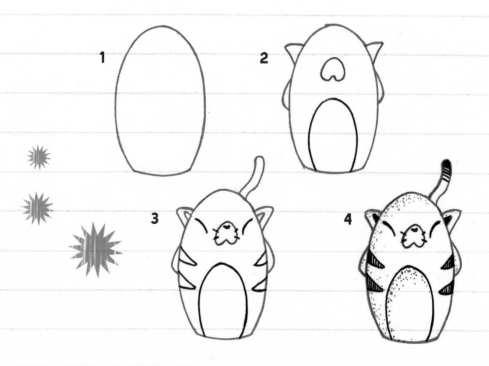

1   2

3   4

SQUIGGLE CREATURE

Draw a loose squiggle shape. Don't think too much about what shape you are drawing. Look at your squiggle. Think where you'd want to position the face first.

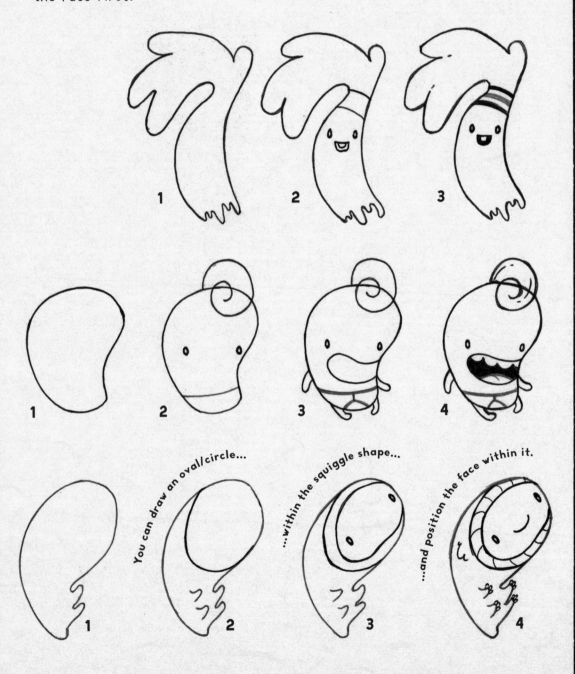

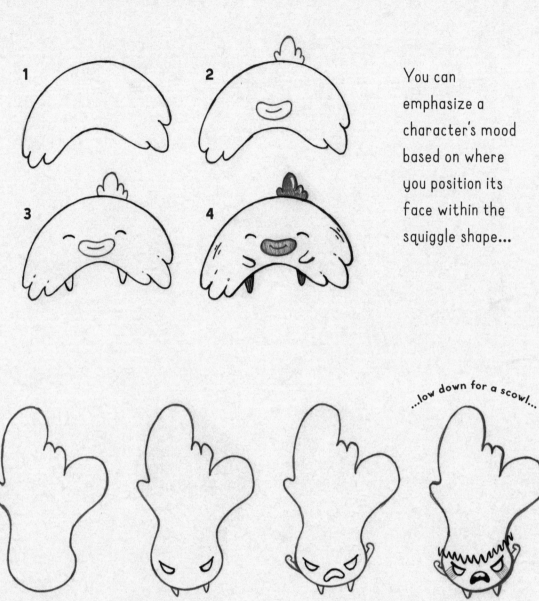

You can emphasize a character's mood based on where you position its face within the squiggle shape...

...low down for a scowl...

...high up to look gleeful!

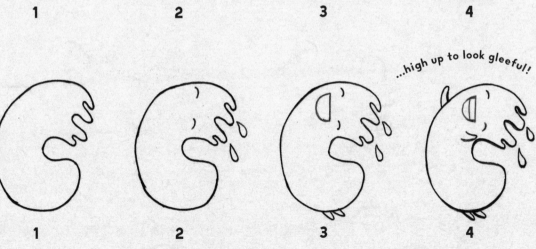

3 IN 1 Create a unique CHARACTER

If you want to create an original character but are stuck for ideas, picking different types of reference can help get the creative juices flowing!

For example, pick three random things from three different categories, e.g.:

- **FOOD**
- **PROFESSION**
- **MAN-MADE OBJECT**

er...

1

er....lightbulb-leek?!

2

A lightbulb-leek....and erm....of course...

3

...it's a leek-lightbulb-cowboy!

4

Yes, you've guessed it. It's an ice lolly-cactus-ballet dancer, melting in the desert sun!

1

2

3

4

Tip

Start simple. Pick a single object to make the body shape. Then add to it with the two other objects/themes you have chosen.

STACK THEM UP

Practice drawing simple shapes...

...stack them up...

...and up...and up...and up!

important!

Tip

With all drawings, make sure you draw at a scale you're comfortable with. You don't want to draw your object only to find that adding detail is too fiddly because you are working with too small an outline.

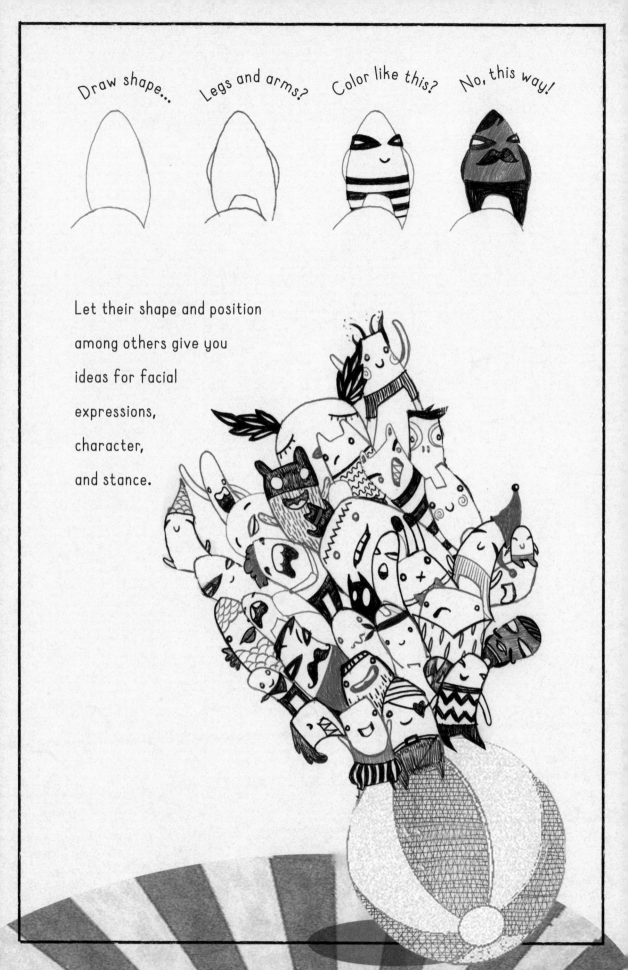

Draw shape... Legs and arms? Color like this? No, this way!

Let their shape and position among others give you ideas for facial expressions, character, and stance.

Ceaseless CITYSCAPE

Draw a stack-them-up cityscape using basic cuboid shapes:

Put that ruler down—no need to be precise!

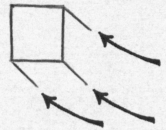

Try to keep these three lines parallel to one another.

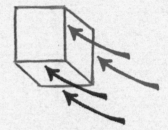

Try to keep all the horizontal and vertical lines parallel to their counterparts.

STACK THEM UP LIKE BUILDING BLOCKS

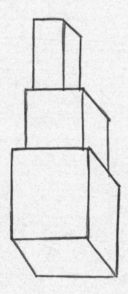

Start with the bigger-sized cuboids at the bottom. They gradually get smaller as they stack up. See how the bottom box is complete but those stacked above have lines that stop before they cross over the box below. Draw all the cubes using red pen, as some lines will cross over and you might want to cover them up by shading in a darker color.

Tip

Draw the facing square/rectangle of your cuboid first and then the diagonal lines.

KEEP ON BUILDING

There will be shading-in later, so draw over each
line a couple of times to make them stand out.

If you draw a larger box on top of a smaller one,
here's how to finish the cuboid shape.

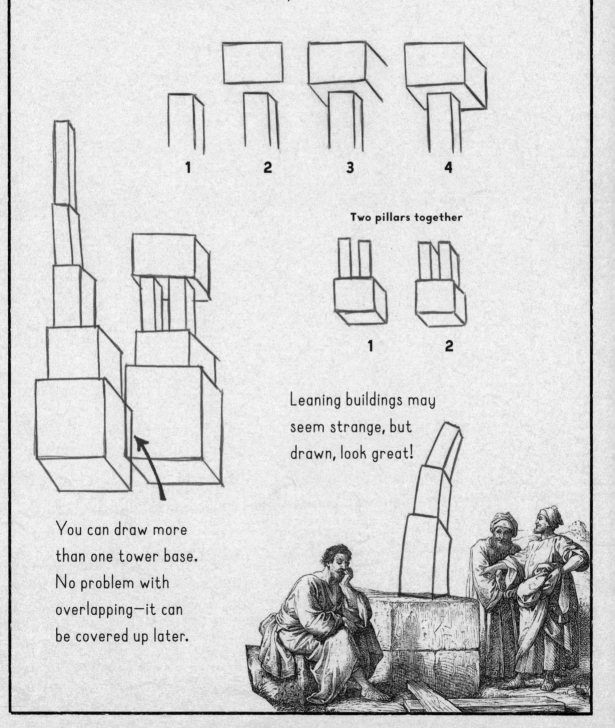

1   **2**   **3**   **4**

Two pillars together

1   **2**

Leaning buildings may
seem strange, but
drawn, look great!

You can draw more
than one tower base.
No problem with
overlapping—it can
be covered up later.

Simple *windows*...

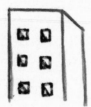

Different windows with different *reflections*...

**Diagonal lines
of light**

**Reflection of
buildings opposite**

**Reflection of
clouds passing by**

**Diagonal lines
across multiple
windows**

Adding *shading* to your block buildings can add form and depth. Below are some examples...

**Straight lines:
Parallel to the outlines
of the building**

**Cross-hatched lines: Parallel
to the outlines of the building**

**Stippling:
For the very
patient!**

You can draw buildings behind your front row of buildings. It's best to keep them larger, with simple, light shading so the cityscape doesn't become too busy and confusing.

FUNNY FACES

When creating funny faces, think about *extremes*:

· extreme size of the facial features

· extreme position of facial features

· extreme facial feature shapes

· extreme expressions

· extreme hair

For these faces I've drawn a basic oval shape, then added the features, thinking about the extremes listed above—e.g. if they have small eyes/nose, I give then a large mouth; or big hair with tiny features.

You can create humor with crazy accessories. Here are a couple of step-by-step examples...

You could use a circle stencil for this one!

FUNNY FACES

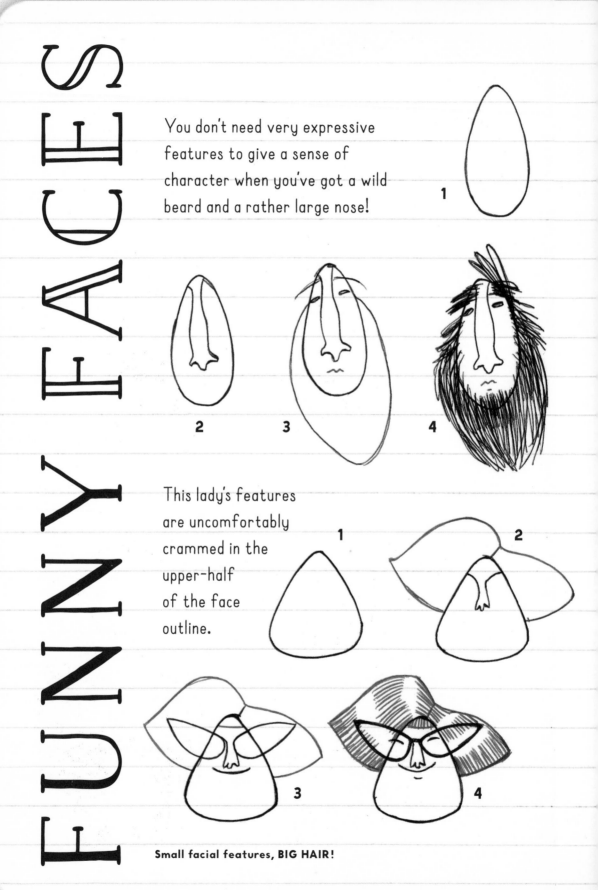

You don't need very expressive features to give a sense of character when you've got a wild beard and a rather large nose!

1

2

3

4

This lady's features are uncomfortably crammed in the upper-half of the face outline.

1

2

3

4

Small facial features, BIG HAIR!

You can create funny faces by basing the shape of the face on an object. Only draw the outline of the object though, and save the detail for the face.

A sock...

...calls for a big chin!

A mushroom shape...

...must have a wide smile!

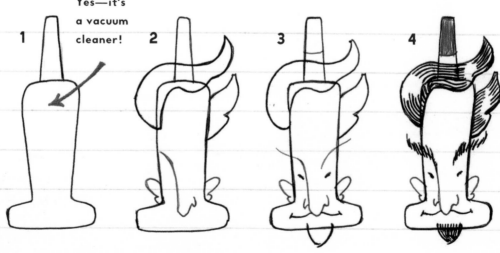

Yes—it's a vacuum cleaner!

HATCHING, SCUMBLING, & STIPPLING

Unlike with pencil, it is difficult to add tonal value (that is, make darker) to your drawing just by increasing the pressure you apply to your pen. You can, however, add tone by using specific strokes. Below are some popular techniques.

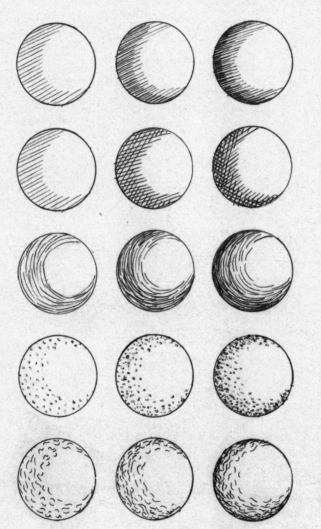

HATCHING:
Rows of parallel lines

CROSS-HATCHING:
Rows of straight lines, crossing over one another

CONTOUR-HATCHING:
Contoured lines that follow the outline of the shape, adding over one another

STIPPLING:
Using dots ... and lots of them!

SCUMBLING:
Using scribbled marks

WARNING: *Too much stippling and scumbling could make your eyes go squiffy!*

HERE ARE SOME EXAMPLES OF HOW YOU CAN APPLY VALUE

Hatching is good for adding form and depth to solid, unmoving structures.

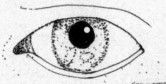

Stippling provides a smooth but finely textured surface to objects.

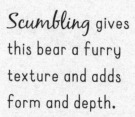

Scumbling gives this bear a furry texture and adds form and depth.

Employ a mixture of textures to portray different surfaces and add depth...

TEXTURES

Here are some textures you can try out in pen. There are endless kinds to create. Take inspiration from nature, man-made materials, and so on, then draw an object, character, or scene, and fill them in. There are no rules. *Have fun and experiment!*

HERE ARE SOME WAYS TO APPLY YOUR TEXTURES

You can keep it simple and apply textures/ patterns that relate to the object itself.

You can add them to various solid forms...

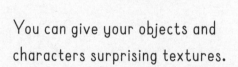

Block letters (see pages 100–103 for more letters)

Abstract shapes/doodles

You can give your objects and characters surprising textures.

Not amused!

Fantastically Furry

There are many ways to create a furry texture in pen. Below are some step-by-step examples, modeled by a little beastie on the opposite page.

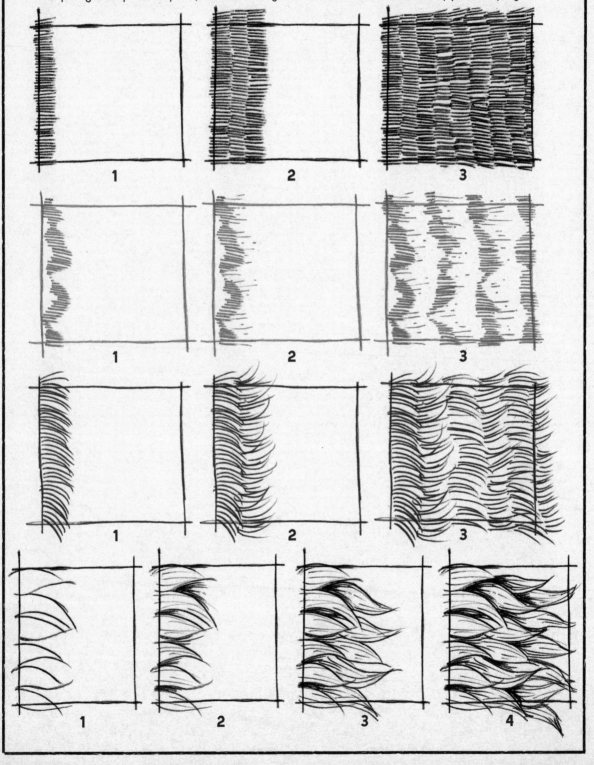

The direction of the fur curves around with the shape of the body. This can add volume to the character. You could also add additional layers of fur around the edge of the body for extra depth. See also page 36 for more on adding texture.

Abominable beastie

Fierce beastie

Werewolf beastie

Nocturnal beastie

FEATHERY *Fun*

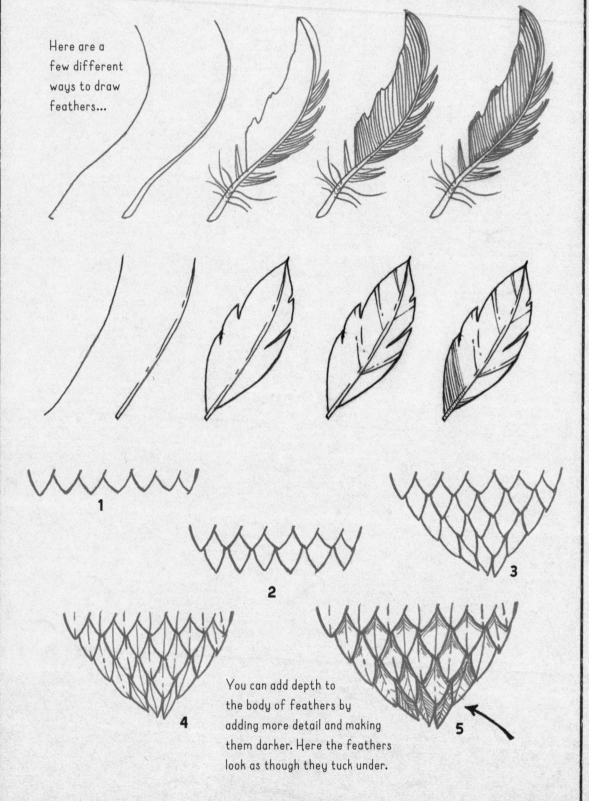

Here are a few different ways to draw feathers...

1

2

3

4

5

You can add depth to the body of feathers by adding more detail and making them darker. Here the feathers look as though they tuck under.

Coming in to land!

1

2

3

Don't get bogged down with too many detailed feathers. Instead imply feather texture with just a few marks, and use detailed feathers sparingly within your character.

4

5

STUPENDOUS SCALES

Below are some simple ways to suggest scales using pen. You can mix the different versions together to great effect.

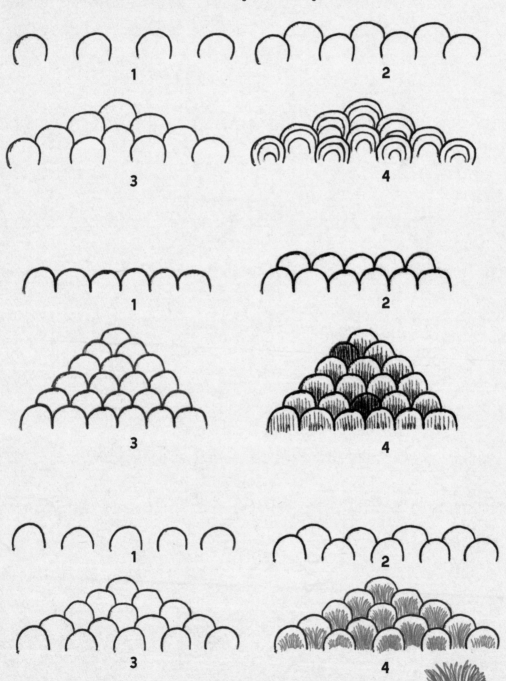

Here, I've given this fangtooth
fish a scaly makeover.
Lets face it—he needed it!
Don't put your pen
too close though,

He might bite!!

1

2

3

HAIR
HERE

Ballpoint pen lends itself very well to drawing hair in many styles, from the realistic to the cartoon. Hair ... sorry ... *here* are some step-by-step samples to get you started.

THIN UNBROKEN LINES WITH A THICK OUTLINE:

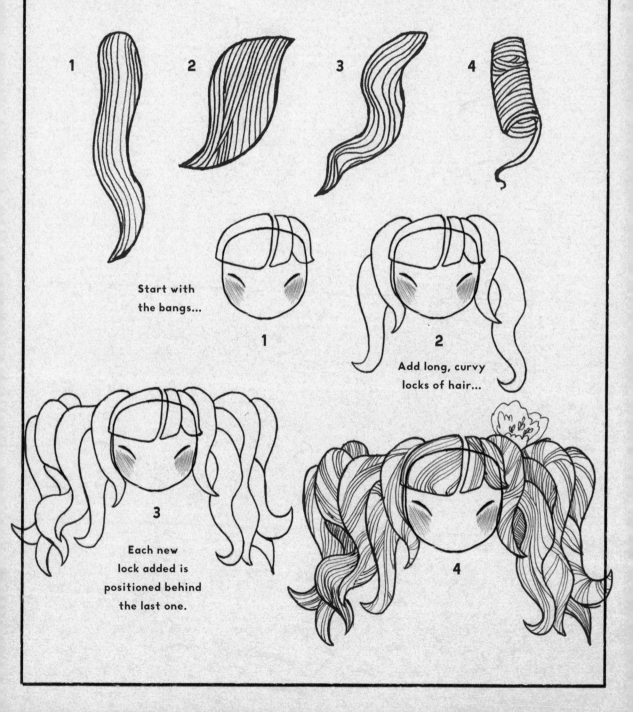

1   2   3   4

Start with the bangs...

1

Add long, curvy locks of hair...

2

Each new lock added is positioned behind the last one.

3

4

PARALLEL GRAPHIC LINES:

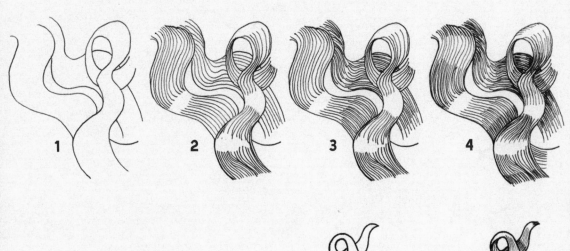

1   2   3   4

Draw some swirls...

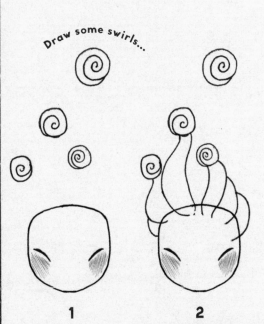

1   2   3   4

| | Connect locks of hair to each swirl... | Then add further locks behind them... | Add shadows beneath each swirl and the overlapping locks. |

HAIR THERE

REALISTIC LOOSE BROKEN LINE:

Draw fewer lines to create highlights, where the braided hair bulges.

Drawing braids can be tricky. Imagine an invisible line of a single lock being braided, as shown here by the arrow. It will help you to position each section as you add them.

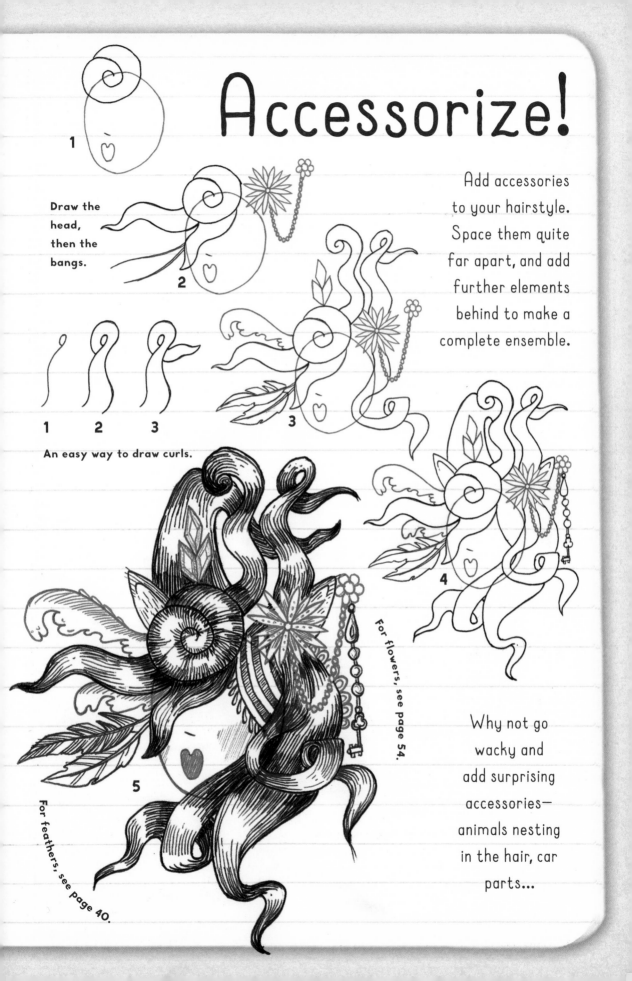

Accessorize!

1

Draw the head, then the bangs.

2

An easy way to draw curls.

1 **2** **3**

3

3

4

5

Add accessories to your hairstyle. Space them quite far apart, and add further elements behind to make a complete ensemble.

For flowers, see page 54.

For feathers, see page 40.

Why not go wacky and add surprising accessories—animals nesting in the hair, car parts...

BATTY BEARDS

Moustaches and beards are all the rage. Drawing faces can be daunting, but including facial hair can really help you tackle it *head on*...

 1

Close up: draw a central curl from under the bottom lip.

 2

As you add more, overlap them, but try not to cross over lines. Draw over each lock a second time to thicken the line.

3

Draw a line down through the middle of each curl.

 **4**

Add a drop shadow below each curl.

Here are two step-by-step renderings of ballpoint beards, modeled by a couple of well-known beardy types!

 **1**

Draw a moustache outline, followed by the beard.

Add locks Downward and outward, not crossing over lines

 **2**

Keep filling in...

3

The curls fill the curves of the beard outline

 **4**

Draw moustache then beard...

1

2

Tip

Make sure you don't draw the white highlight shapes too narrow. If they are not wide enough, they will disappear when you fill in the space around them in solid black.

3

Hairy faces rock!!!

4

Red arrow: Shadows are created by drawing fewer white highlights in that area.

You don't have to use traditional hair textures to create the beards...

1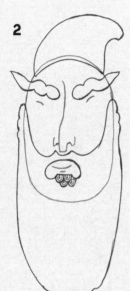

Draw a face shape big enough to include a detailed pattern beard. Then add the features.

Leave a good space between the bottom of the nose and the top lip...

2

Add your beard outline. You can add patterns to eyebrows and hair too!

3

As shown in steps 2 and 3, slowly build up the overlapping pattern in a downward direction.

Close-up of the pattern:

1  **2** 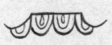 **3**

Why stick with hair or abstract patterns!?

Tip Choose a very simple object or creature shape. It will become a lot more complex when you come to overlap them.

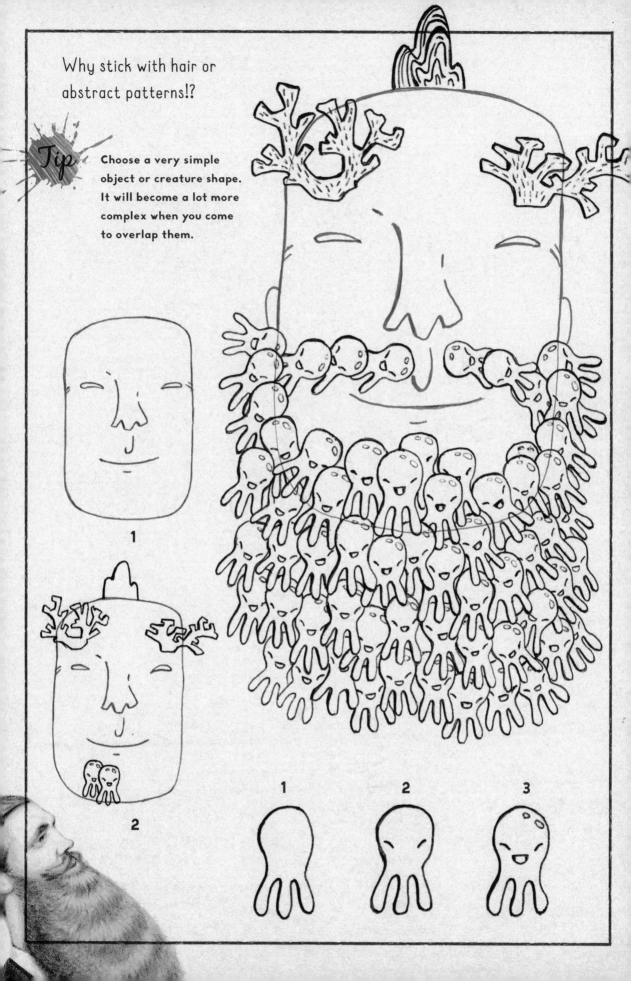

1

2

1   2   3

ALIEN INKCOUNTERS

These creatures need to be *out of this world,* so start by drawing an abstract shape for the body and head.

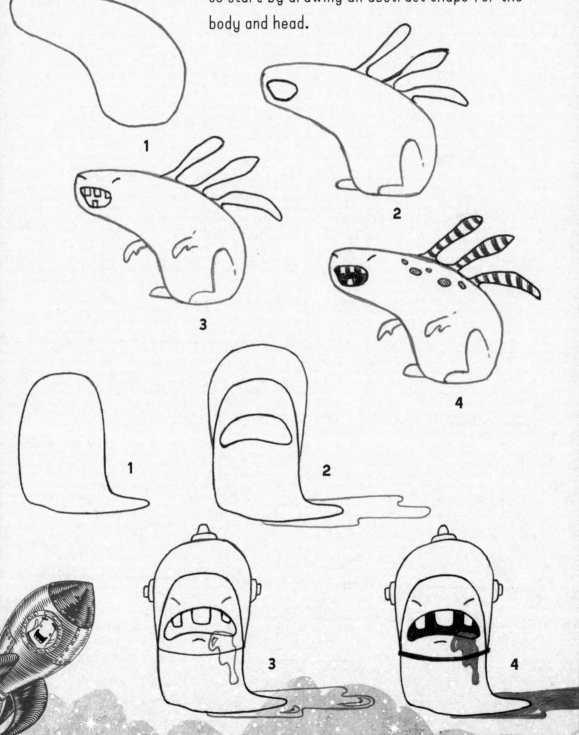

1

2

3

4

1

2

3

4

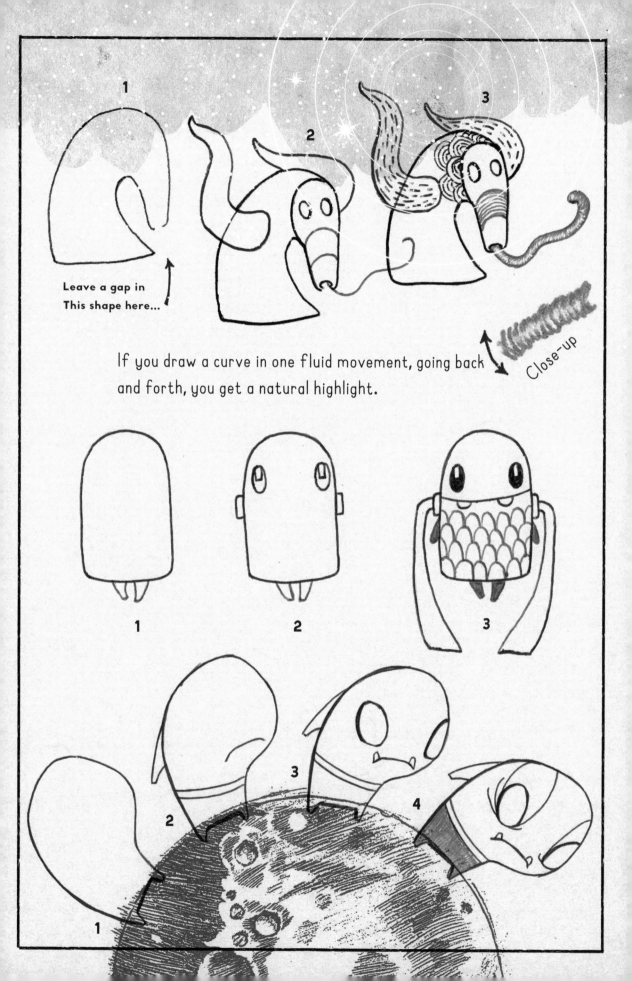

Leave a gap in
This shape here...

If you draw a curve in one fluid movement, going back and forth, you get a natural highlight.

Close-up

Flower POWER!

Here are some flowers to draw and repeat. They are not as complicated as they look. Just take one step at a time...

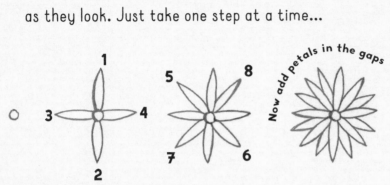

Now add petals in the gaps

Draw the petals in the order they are numbered above. This helps you to position them evenly.

Add a pattern to the petals and vines.

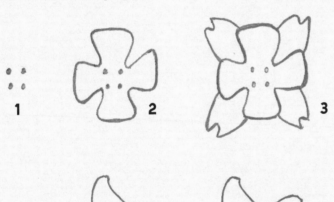

All these flowers are drawn freehand. Don't let wonky petals worry you!

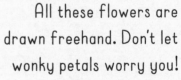

Then you can repeat
the flowers you've
practiced to create
real *flower power!*

DRAW &
MULTIPLY

Here we'll create a patterned image of small objects. Keep them simple—they'll start to look great as you draw them over and over...

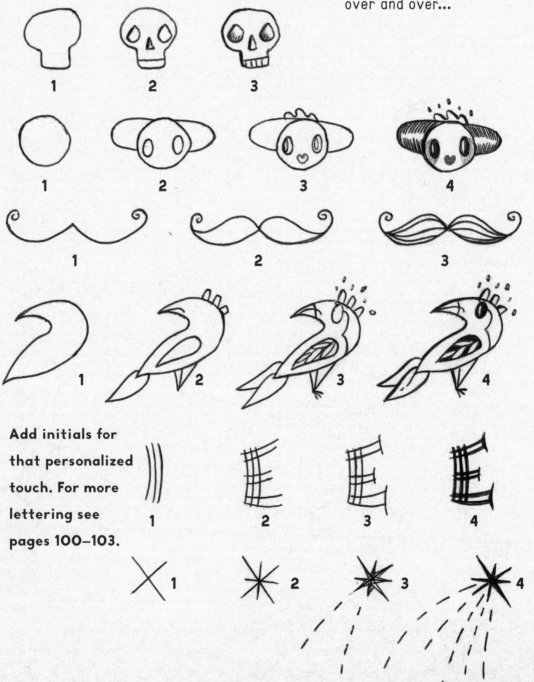

Add initials for that personalized touch. For more lettering see pages 100–103.

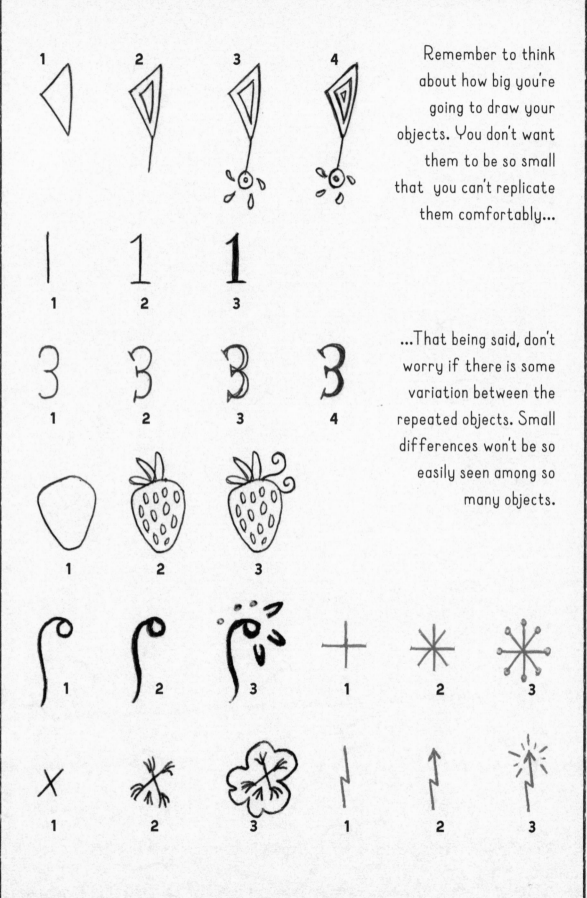

Remember to think about how big you're going to draw your objects. You don't want them to be so small that you can't replicate them comfortably...

...That being said, don't worry if there is some variation between the repeated objects. Small differences won't be so easily seen among so many objects.

You could do your own draw-and-multiply on plain parcel paper or white paper and use it to wrap a present in style (with matching color ribbon). Or decorate an envelope—don't forget to leave space for the stamp!

Rotate the objects as you draw them so that they are at various angles.

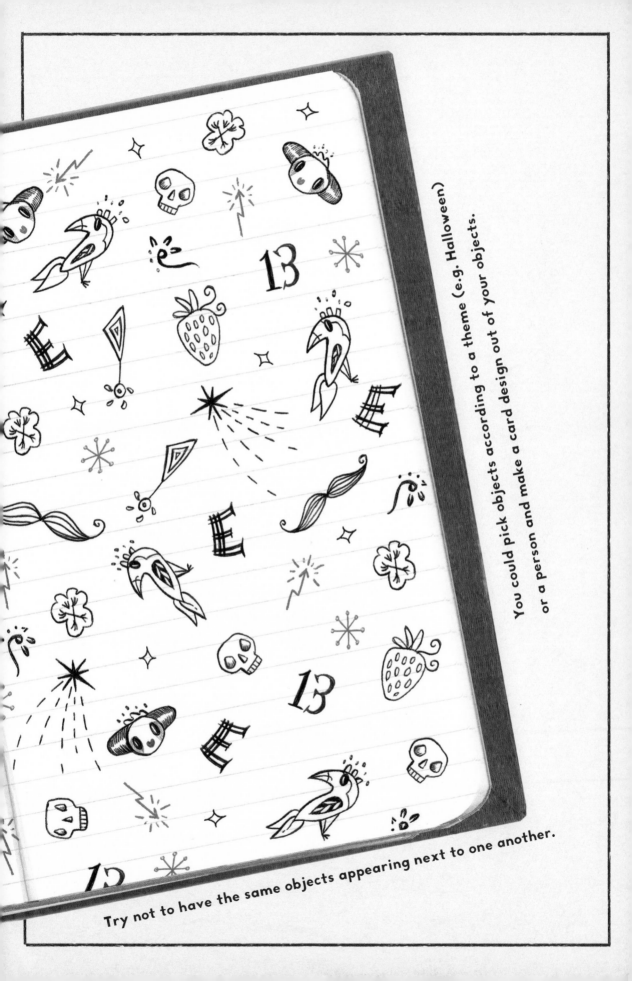

You could pick objects according to a theme (e.g. Halloween) or a person and make a card design out of your objects.

Try not to have the same objects appearing next to one another.

Do a Doodle!

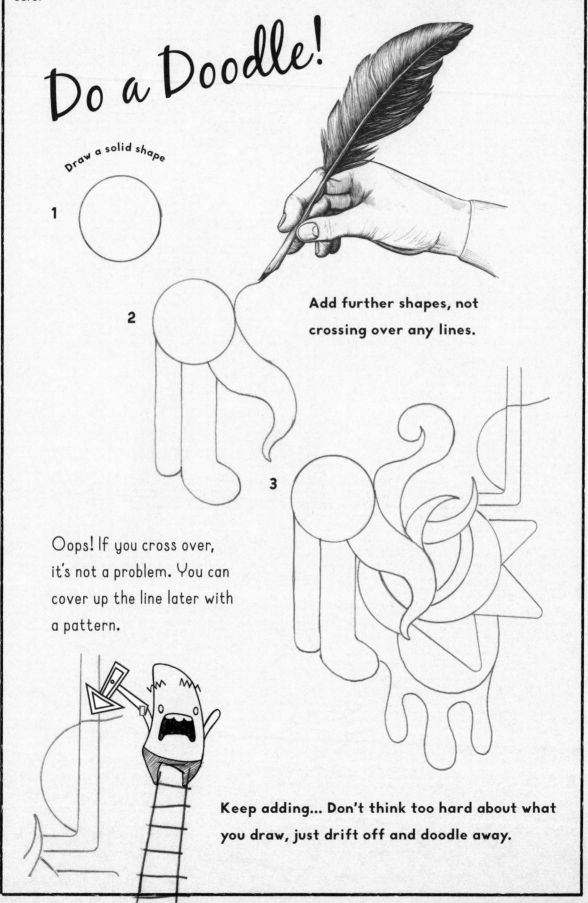

Draw a solid shape

1

2

Add further shapes, not crossing over any lines.

3

Oops! If you cross over, it's not a problem. You can cover up the line later with a pattern.

Keep adding... Don't think too hard about what you draw, just drift off and doodle away.

You can draw freehand or draw
around objects. Can you spot a pair
of scissors handles in my drawing?

Now color in! You can add doodles inside and outside the original outline.

Name:

Form:

Subject:

I think the teacher would approve!

You could also try making a themed doodle. For example, draw outlines of Christmas decorations and fill in the shapes with Christmas-themed patterns (snowflakes, candy cane, paper chains, etc.).

Warning: If you've not got a lot of patience, turn over the page now!

Dotty ABOUT ART DECO

Art Deco is a decorative art developed in the 1920s (a long time ago to you and me!). Ballpoint lends itself well to this style, as Art Deco uses sharply defined outlines, that look great drawn in pen.

Draw around a playing card

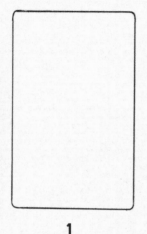

1

Use a ruler and circle stencil To create shaped sections

2

Keep filling, not crossing over existing lines.

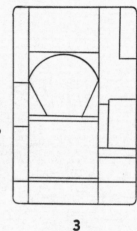

3

That's enough sections!

4

Now fill in the spaces with art deco line-work. Some lines are freehand, some use the ruler and stencil.

The following phrases are good to look up on the internet for some Art Deco inspiration:

- **ART DECO WINDOWS**
- **ART DECO LINES**
- **ART DECO PATTERNS**
- **ART DECO OBJECTS**

Tip

When drawing
fiddly things,
always take a
moment to step
back from your
drawing and see
how it's developing.

You can carefully
cut out the centre
and use your
artwork as a
picture frame.

Add appendages
to the playing
card outline.

Personalize by including
a name or initials.

Line an
ARTISTIC LANDSCAPE

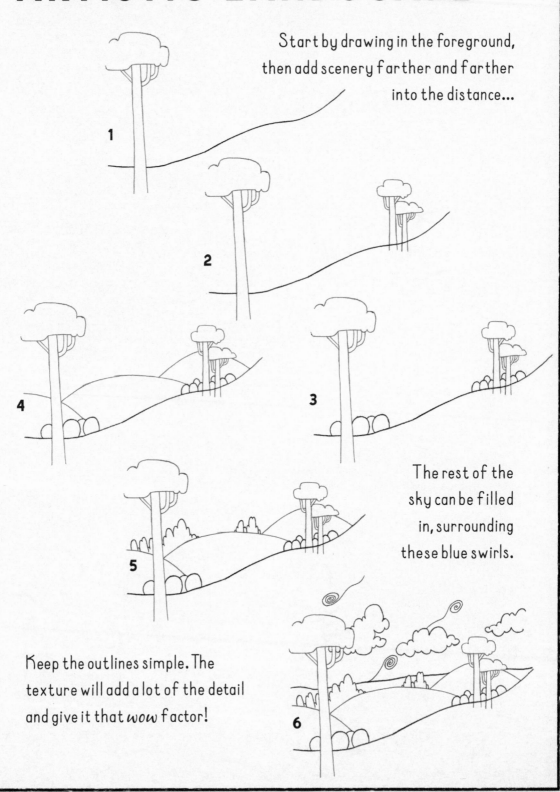

Start by drawing in the foreground, then add scenery farther and farther into the distance...

1

2

4

3

The rest of the sky can be filled in, surrounding these blue swirls.

5

Keep the outlines simple. The texture will add a lot of the detail and give it that *wow* factor!

6

Fill in with simple line textures, that you feel suit the specific object (e.g. a tree trunk=straight vertical lines). Only use one type of texture for each object, otherwise your drawing will become confusing to the eye.

Picture Perfect BORDERS

How you frame a picture can be as important as the picture itself. Whether it's for a photo or a drawing, here are some ways to pen a decorative border in ballpoint.

Simple borders using a straight line:

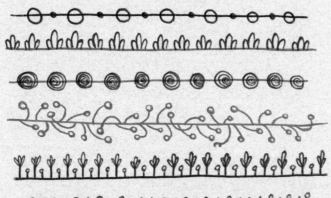

Close-up of leaves with steps

1

2

3

Draw a line...

Add alternately short and long stems either side...

Add circles to the long stems and leaves to the short stems...

Then add the small red stems between each blue stem...

Then draw some little red embellishments...You're done!

Simple frames drawn in a loose style:

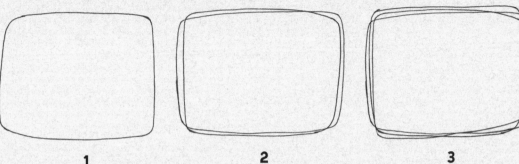

1 **2** **3**

Embellish with decorative shapes...

...Nature...

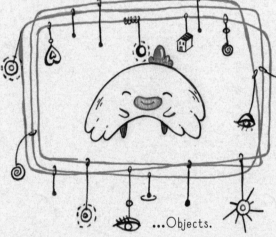

...Objects.

Turn the page to see how to make the ornate frame below, and find fancy letters on pages 100–103.

Tip You can draw your border directly onto a pre-cut picture mount frame.

ORNATE
BORDERS:

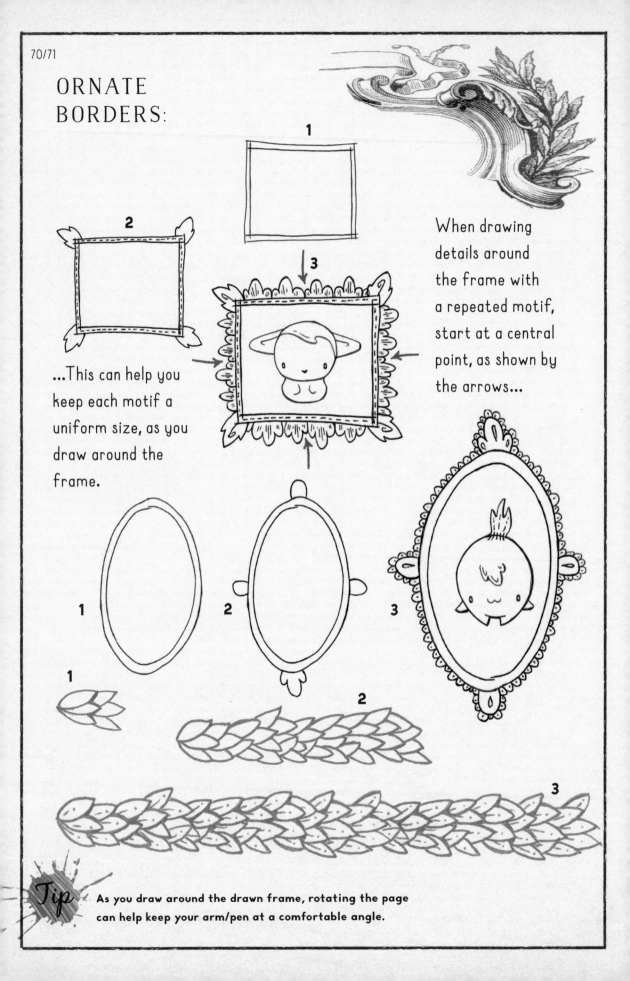

1

2

3

When drawing
details around
the frame with
a repeated motif,
start at a central
point, as shown by
the arrows...

...This can help you
keep each motif a
uniform size, as you
draw around the
frame.

1

2

3

1

1

2

3

Tip As you draw around the drawn frame, rotating the page
can help keep your arm/pen at a comfortable angle.

BUILD-THEM-UP BORDERS:

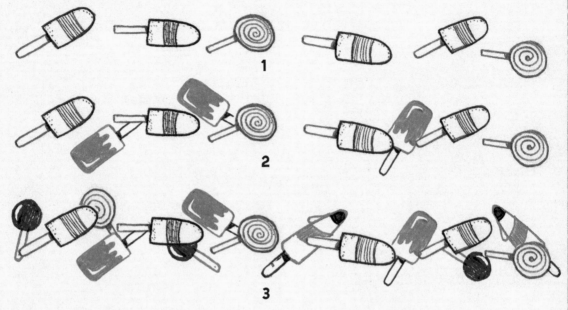

1

2

3

Lollipops for a summery feel...

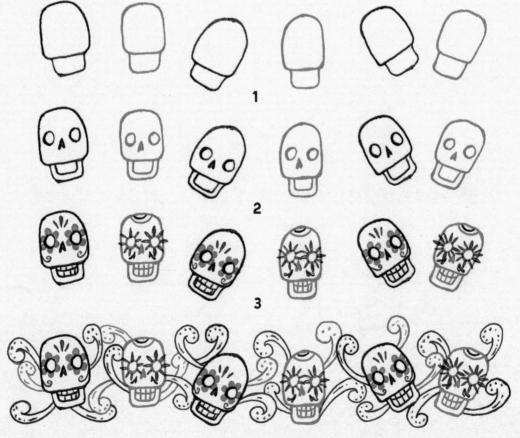

1

2

3

4

...Day of the Dead for spooky fun!

Faces border.

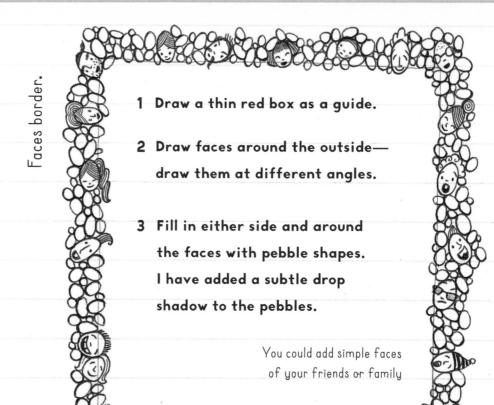

1 Draw a thin red box as a guide.

2 Draw faces around the outside—
   draw them at different angles.

3 Fill in either side and around
   the faces with pebble shapes.
   I have added a subtle drop
   shadow to the pebbles.

You could add simple faces
of your friends or family

Design an
abstract shape
and repeat:

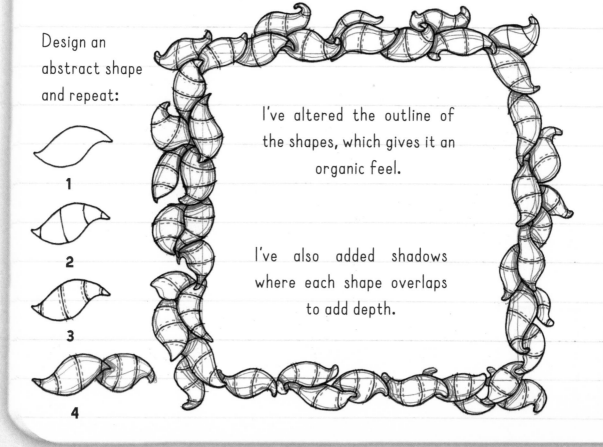

I've altered the outline of
the shapes, which gives it an
organic feel.

I've also added shadows
where each shape overlaps
to add depth.

1

2

3

4

BETWEEN THE LINES:

Draw freehand or around a frame, then fill in with a pattern.

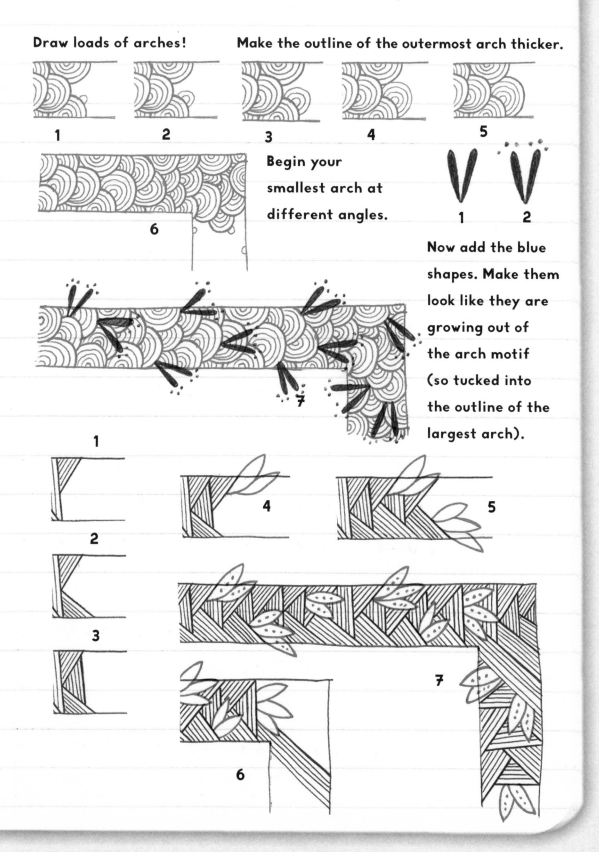

Draw loads of arches!   **Make the outline of the outermost arch thicker.**

1   2   3   4   5

6

Begin your smallest arch at different angles.

1   2

Now add the blue shapes. Make them look like they are growing out of the arch motif (so tucked into the outline of the largest arch).

7

1

2

3

4

5

6

7

PATTERNS *in Pen...*

1

2

3

4

5

6

7

You've already seen some basic patterns in the Textures section of this book (pages 36-37). Patterns can comprise of absolutely anything—for example simple mark-making, shapes, objects, animals, etc.—as long as it is a repeated design.

Let's start with an abstract pattern.

Here are steps for the two more complex patterns from the design below.

1

2

3

Patterns by definition are a repeated design but drawing in pen only doesn't allow us to be precise. So I'm going to draw freehand and not worry about winning prizes for accuracy!

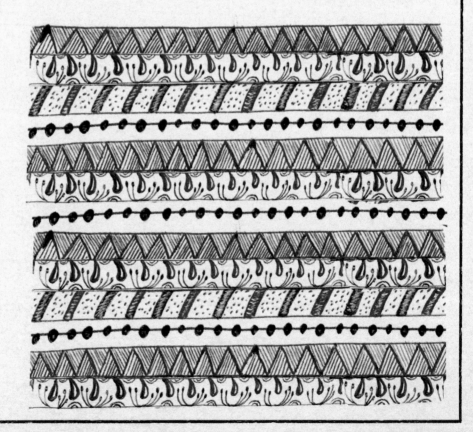

NATURE:

Draw parallel wavy lines.

1

Draw two leaves
on every bend.
Thicken the outline.

2

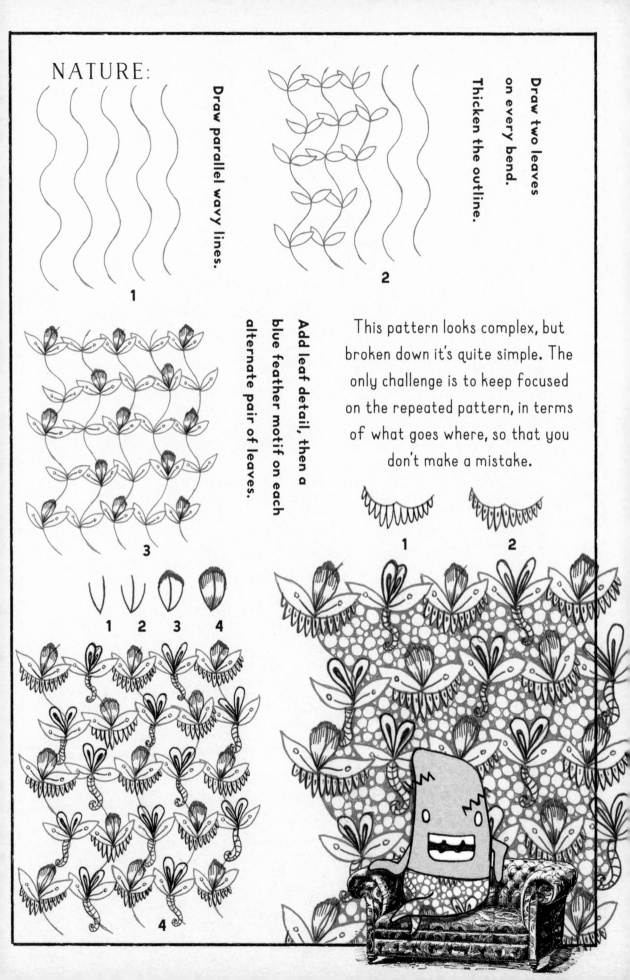

Add leaf detail, then a
blue feather motif on each
alternate pair of leaves.

3

This pattern looks complex, but broken down it's quite simple. The only challenge is to keep focused on the repeated pattern, in terms of what goes where, so that you don't make a mistake.

1   **2**

1   **2**   **3**   **4**

4

Drawing a grid first can help give you confidence to tackle a repeated pattern...

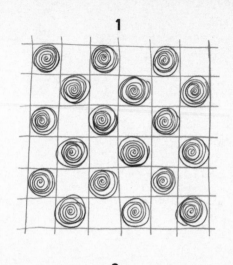

1

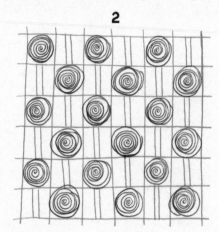

2

It can be fun not to plan what you are going to draw before you start. Draw different abstract shapes and repeat, to see what you end up with!

I added shadow beneath lollipop.

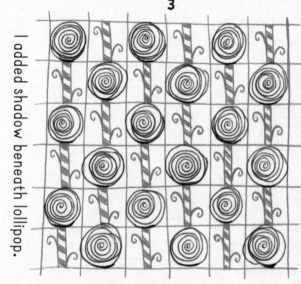

3

Swirl to give impact.

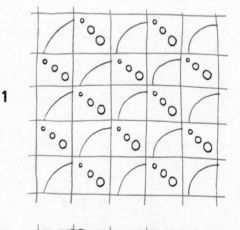

1

3

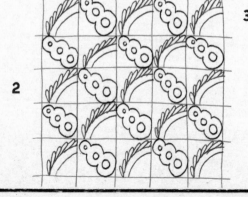

2

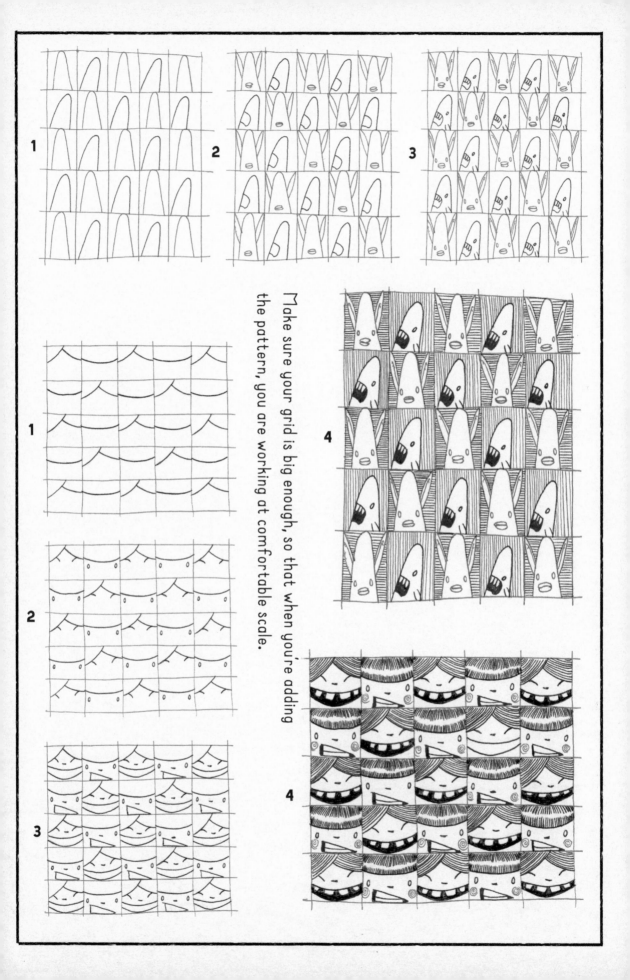

Make sure your grid is big enough, so that when you're adding the pattern, you are working at comfortable scale.

PATTERNS: PLAYING WITH VALUE AND SHADOWS...

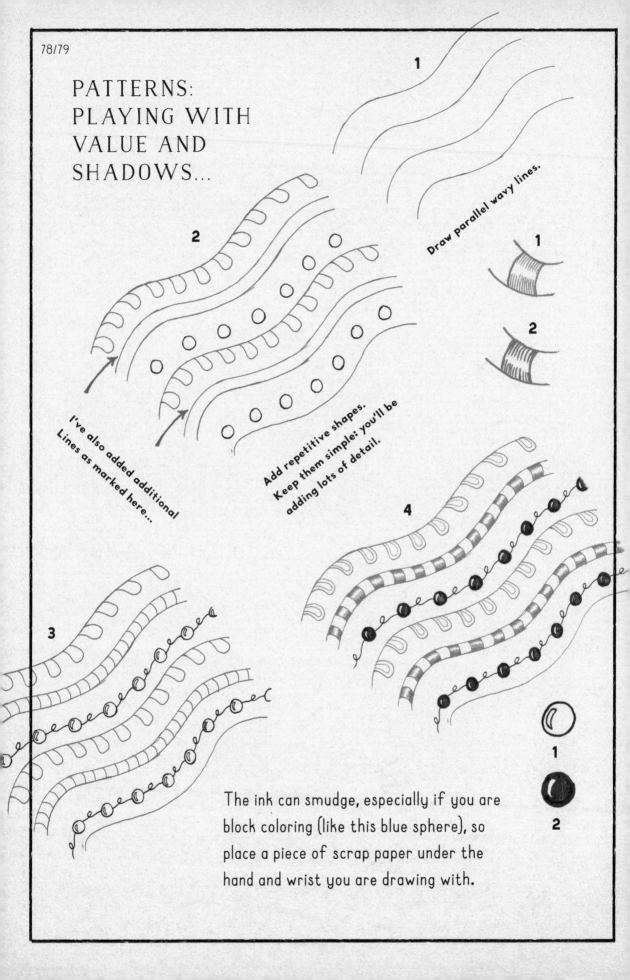

1

Draw parallel wavy lines.

2

I've also added additional Lines as marked here...

Add repetitive shapes. Keep them simple; you'll be adding lots of detail.

1

2

3

4

1

2

The ink can smudge, especially if you are block coloring (like this blue sphere), so place a piece of scrap paper under the hand and wrist you are drawing with.

5

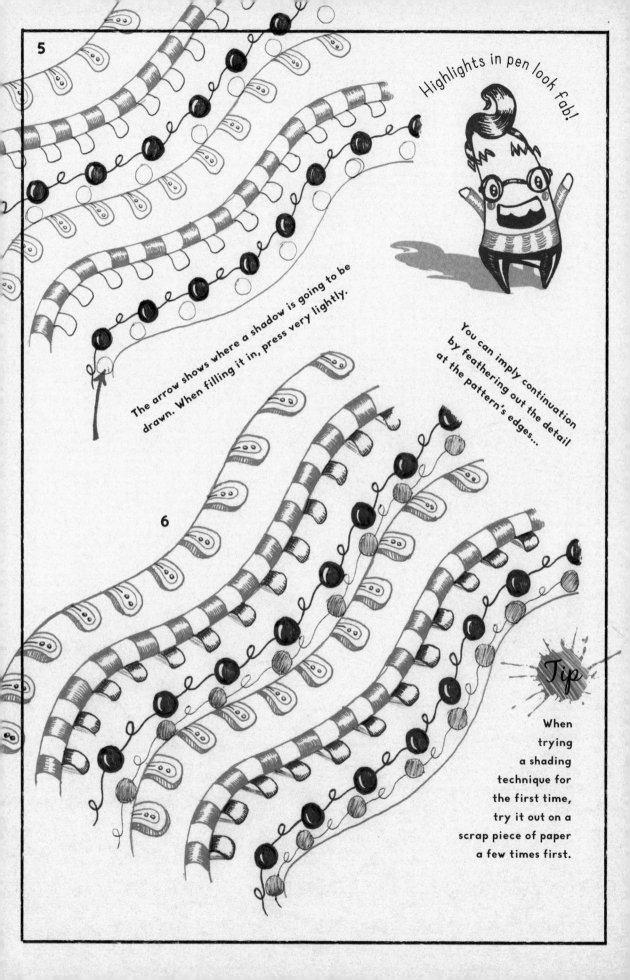

Highlights in pen look fab!

The arrow shows where a shadow is going to be drawn. When filling it in, press very lightly.

You can imply continuation by feathering out the detail at the pattern's edges...

6

Tip

When trying a shading technique for the first time, try it out on a scrap piece of paper a few times first.

Ink on Print

Ballpoint can look great when applied to the printed page (with permission from the owner of course!).

Ballpoint ink sits best on smooth matte paper. If you want to photocopy the text, rather than draw directly onto the page, photocopy paper also works well.

Blocking in areas in solid color works well on a printed page. It also helps make your drawing not get lost among a busy text background.

Pick a Scene...

1 Such a romantic scene.........

It's making me a little queasy!

2 It needs something.........

Mmm... One moment.....

Draw something that conflicts with the printed picture. A peaceful scene? Add a chaotic/ scary creature. A dramatic scene? Add a character looking very calm etc.

3

...Much better!!

PICK SOME WORDS...

To inspire character design...

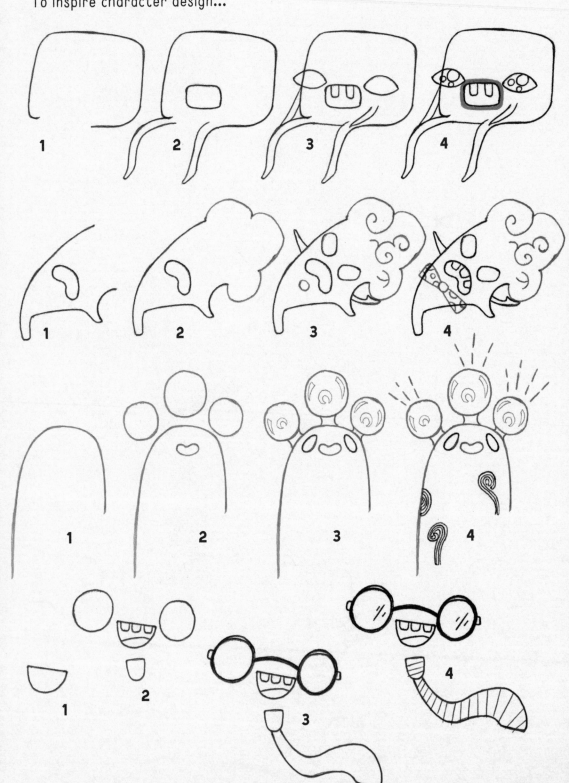

But, because they are vibrations, science invented the idea of something that would vibrate with them and called it the Ether. Sir Isaac Newton was at first inclined to believe that light moved through space in emissions of fine particles, or corpuscles, and therefore in straight lines, and found some objections to the vibrating theory; but he left the question undecided, and his successors interpreted his opinion as being in favour of the corpuscles; and the authority of his name gained the acceptance of his idea for a whole century. Thus was superseded by the wave or undulatory theory which had first been suggested by Huygens, a contemporary of Newton, and was afterwards revived by Thomas Young and, being generally then accepted, the Ether also was born again.

THE VIBRATIONS OF MATTER THAT MAKE US SEE LIGHT

We know nothing about it we can prove. All we really know is that the light waves are transmitted. When they reach the eye after their journey, which may be short or may be immeasurably long, they make an impression on the retina which is sent on to the brain and there makes us conscious of light.

In a general way we may say that the hotter matter is the more likely it is to send out vibrations which, when they hit our eyes, make us see light. For an illustration we may take a piece of black carbon. When cold, it gives out no light and does not reflect much; but heat it up and it first glows red and then as it grows hot, it can be made to give out a white light, as in an electric arc-lamp. In the end it is so hot that it becomes a gas, and contributes its share to the sunlight.

WHAT HAPPENS TO A PIECE OF IRON WHEN IT IS HEATED

A piece of iron would do as well to show what we mean. Cold and solid, it gives out no light from itself; heat it and it glows with a red light; heat it more, and it becomes white-hot and melts into a liquid; heat it further still and it goes into a white-hot gas such as, again, is found in the Sun. Here, then, is an example of three states of iron matter:

The solid state, in which the vibration grows more vigorous as the solid grows hotter;

The liquid state, in which vibration takes place freely;

The gaseous state, in which vibration is still more marked.

It is the same iron always—but why should it vibrate more in one state than in another, and how does it vibrate at all?

The only way to answer that question is to consider the iron, not as a lump, but as built up of something movable, as a house or a wall is built up of bricks. If you glance at one of these coloured pictures, to be found on an advertisement page you will at first imagine it to be made up of solid patches of black and white; but if you examine the dark patches with a magnifying glass you would see that they were built up of multitudes of little dots. All matter is built up in a similar way of tiny bits, but these are so small that no magnifying glass would reveal them. During the last few years new microscopes of tremendous power, using electrons instead of light, and a photographic plate instead of the human eye to "see" with, have revealed something of the tiny fragments of which substances are made, but even these fragments of matter are built up of still tinier fragments which no microscope has yet been powerful enough to reveal.

SPLITTING UP THINGS TILL WE REACH AN INVISIBLE SPECK

We spoke just now of bricks. Suppose we were to pound these to powder. Suppose we were to take a grain of this and split it up again. Even then the fragments would be almost invisible. Even the grains would be made smaller and smaller still. So also with the grains of iron which we could possibly arrive at.

But if we go on in our minds still splitting up and splitting up we can imagine that at last we might arrive at a speck of matter so small that it could not be split up any more. That is what, ever since the time of the Greeks, has been called an Atom—meaning a thing which cannot be cut up into smaller bits.

Now a lump of iron is built of such atoms; the atoms of iron are its bricks. We can get some idea of what happens when the lump of iron grows hot. Its bricks begin to jostle one another; they move about; they vibrate. As the iron grows hotter the vibrations become more powerful and rapid. What happens then?

We can see by a story. Captain Scott told in one of his books how, when he and his companions were on sledge journeys in the Antarctic, after they had packed

---

When drawing highlights, don't try to leave a blank space as you fill in. Instead, draw the main shape, then the outline of the highlight, and fill in around it.

SIMPLE CITYSCAPE

I've found a few photos of buildings I like the look of, from which I'm going to draw a cityscape. This is a lot *simpler*, than it sounds...

I won't be concerned with accuracy or detail. With a few general rules you can create a great 'scape!

1. Draw outline of the building first.

2. Add basic window shapes. I've added a shadow to each window.

3. The only other detail in this case is brickwork at top and bottom of each window.

Place contrasting colors together.

I've drawn a very rough outline of this complex building. I won't score any points for accuracy!

You can overlap buildings. Don't fill in every detail. Leave areas blank to prevent your drawing from looking confusing. Suggest windows with simple marks, such as straight lines...

Put smaller buildings in the foreground and big ones, like skyscrapers, toward the back. You can add just a tad more of the finer details to the foreground buildings. Make sure the building outlines clearly overlap, rather than sit on top of one another.

Marvellous Motion!

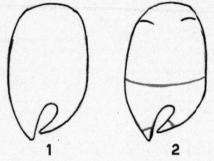

Adding movement can really bring your drawing to life.

1

2

3

4

Falling: Add vertical motion marks. Hair and tutu flying upward.

Blast off!! Hair and tutu forced downward with g-force!

The facial features are moved toward the top of the head, as if she is looking upward.

Trying to fly! Implying motion, by drawing multiple arms.

Spinning around, using oval motion marks.

Remember to keep the arms attached to the shoulder! They should join the body in the same place.

Here, hair is important for showing how the direction of the body and the way it's moving.

I'm a winner!

Head up with confidence, and looking forward. She has her eyes on the prize!

Sad expression, bowed head, and limp arms imply a slow plod...

I'm a loser!!

Oh joy!

Happy expression, with a star jump position

Oh boy!

The position of floor in relation to the figure helps imply motion too.

Create movement with composition...
Simple variations of line can imply form,
depth, distance, and all kinds of movement.

Undulate with me!

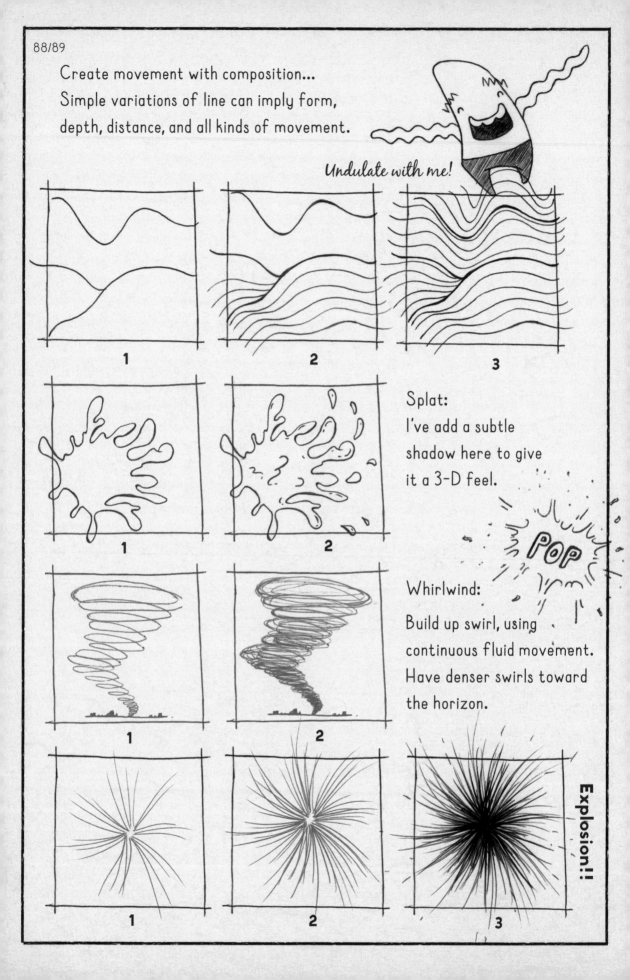

1
2
3

Splat:
I've add a subtle
shadow here to give
it a 3-D feel.

1
2

Whirlwind:
Build up swirl, using
continuous fluid movement.
Have denser swirls toward
the horizon.

1
2

Explosion!!

1
2
3

1

2 Try to make the red curves look as though they are part of the same series of circles.

3

Swirl...

4

1

2

3

4

5

...Slither...

Here the snake-like shapes get bigger as they get nearer. Making use of perspective in this way can also imply movement.

Keeping it simple...

Here are a few tips to help you when drawing from observation.

First, draw the outline. Squinting your eyes while looking at the object can help you simplify how you see its shape.

Then add a few details.

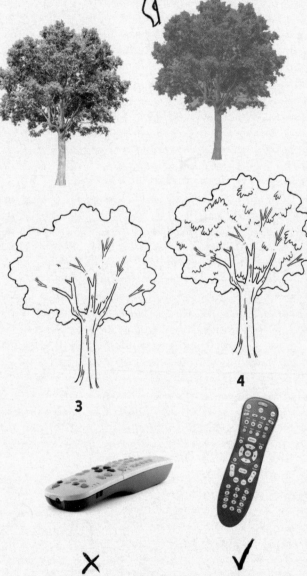

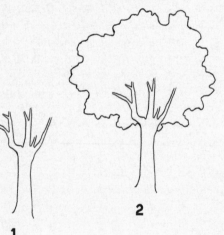

1

2

3

4

The more you draw an object, the better you will get at capturing it. The best way to learn is practice, practice, and you guessed it...

more practice!

✗   ✓

If possible, position the object you're drawing so that you can see its most recognizable features clearly (and draw it from the easiest angle!).

Everything you see can be
simplified into basic shapes.
Try drawing these rough
shapes in your red ballpoint,
and the final outlines in black.

You don't have to include a lot
of detail. Just pick the features
that define the object or scene
the most.

Here, I used textures to
imply detail. I've not drawn
every individual tree! It
can be a good exercise to
limit how much time you
allow yourself to draw a
picture—it's a good way
stop you from over-
drawing the picture.

MONSTERS
INK...

Your folks assure you there are no monsters in your room at night...

...They want you to give them a peaceful evening of course.

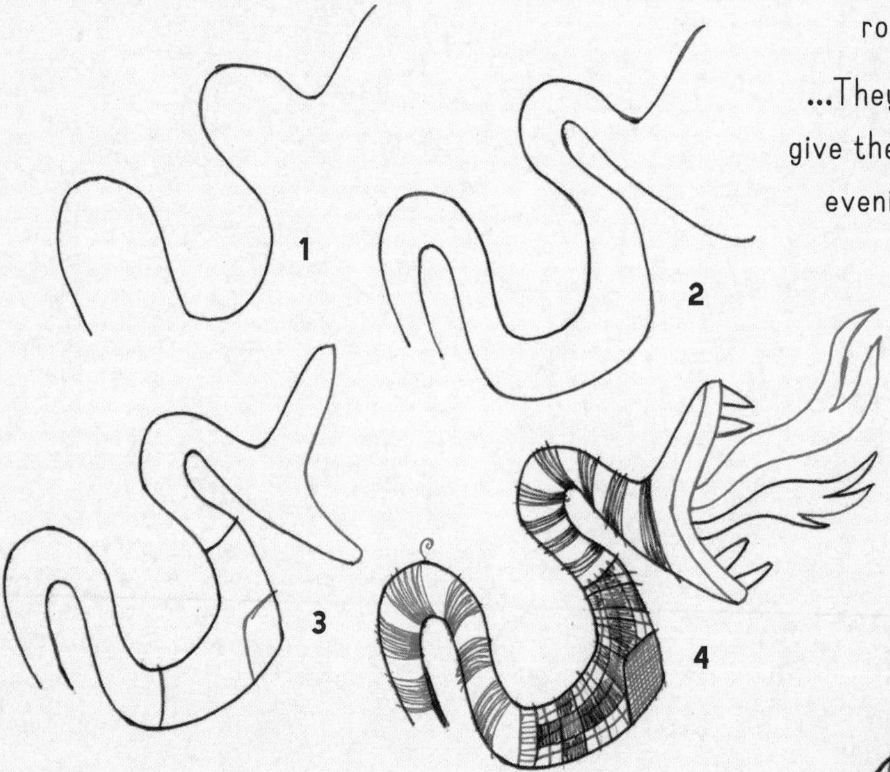

1

2

3

4

Some of dad's socks have found their way into your sock drawer, with *sinister consequences*...

5

Dust bunnies in the corner of your room! ...Almost *too cute* to vacuum up!

1

2

3

4

5

Draw over the main outlines a second time so that they stand out once the furry texture is added.

6

Use scruffy but dense shading around the face, then looser directional shading on the tufty bits. For more fur- and hair- shading techniques see pages 38-39 and 44-47.

7

Could there be a menacing *monster* in your closet??

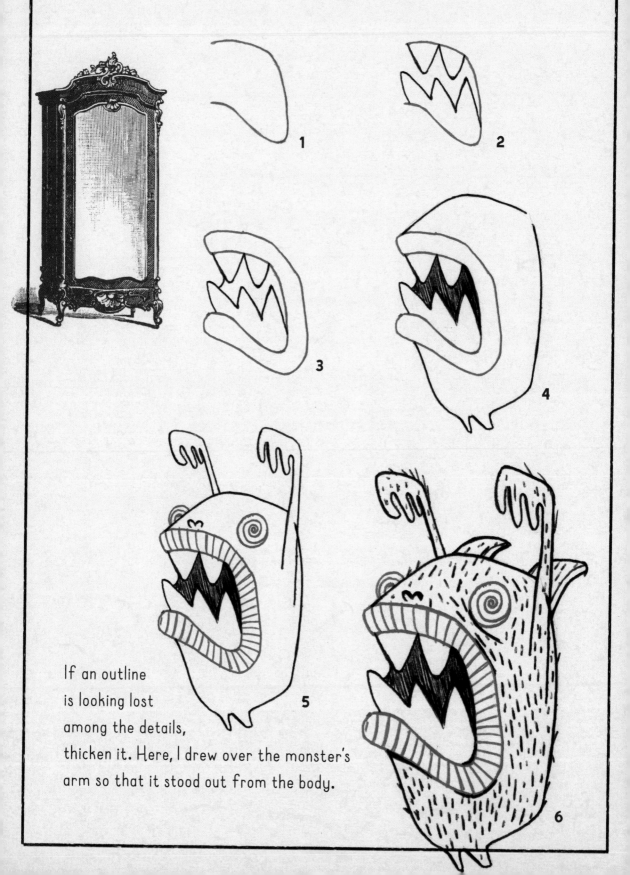

1

2

3

4

5

If an outline
is looking lost
among the details,
thicken it. Here, I drew over the monster's
arm so that it stood out from the body.

6

Who's that snuggling up to you in bed?? It's only the *bed bugs*...
And by the way, they do bite!

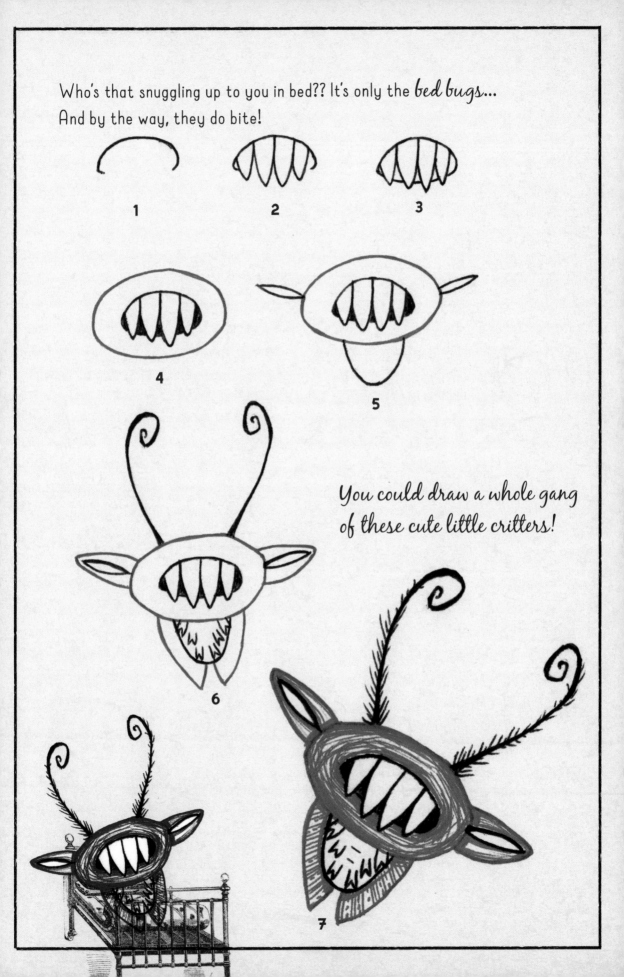

1

2

3

4

5

You could draw a whole gang
of these cute little critters!

6

7

HOW *does your* GARDEN GROW?

Here's a way to create your own unique garden. I've taken inspiration from old engravings of plants and flowers. Create your own genetically engineered array of the weird and wonderful...

When coloring around objects (like the center of this red flower), be sure to draw the shapes large enough, so that they don't disappear when you fill in.

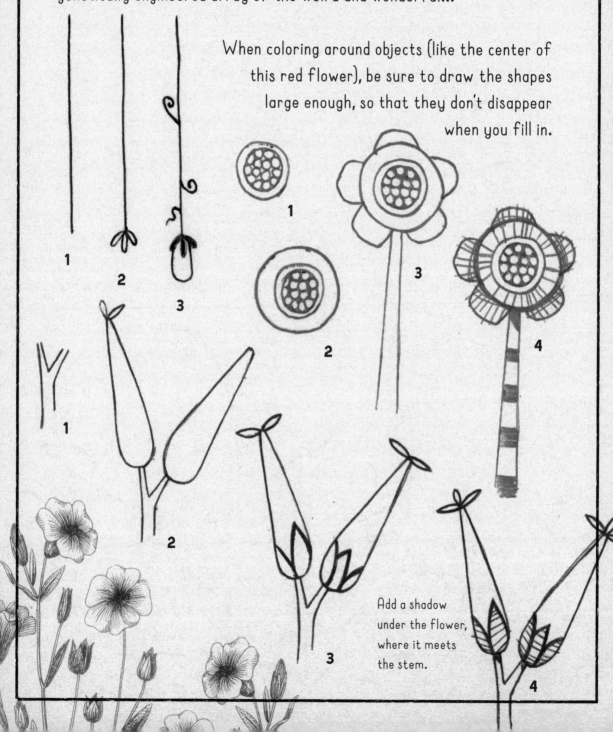

Add a shadow under the flower, where it meets the stem.

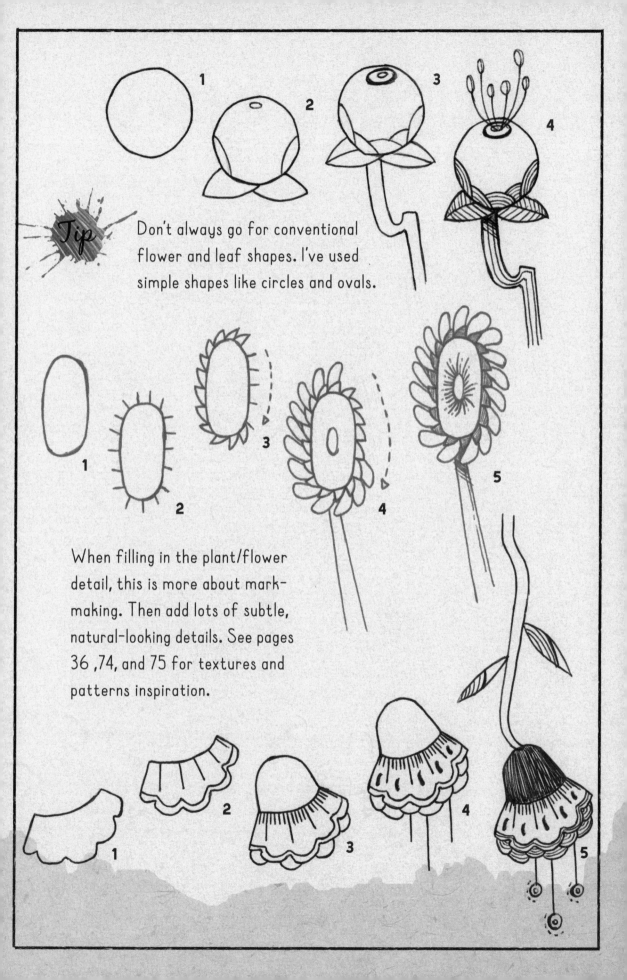

Tip

Don't always go for conventional flower and leaf shapes. I've used simple shapes like circles and ovals.

When filling in the plant/flower detail, this is more about mark-making. Then add lots of subtle, natural-looking details. See pages 36, 74, and 75 for textures and patterns inspiration.

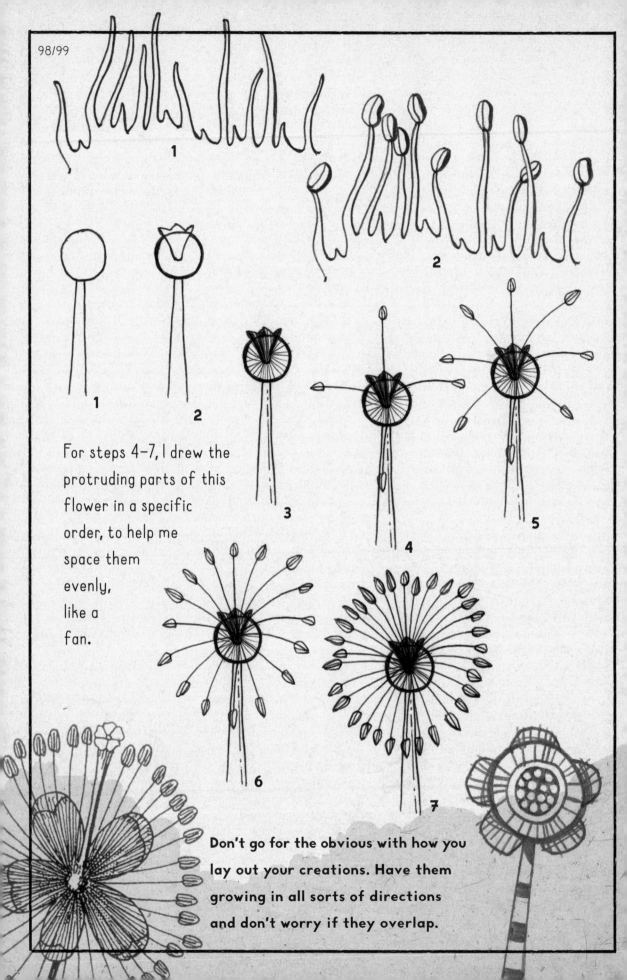

1

2

1

2

For steps 4–7, I drew the
protruding parts of this
flower in a specific
order, to help me
space them
evenly,
like a
fan.

3

4

5

6

7

**Don't go for the obvious with how you
lay out your creations. Have them
growing in all sorts of directions
and don't worry if they overlap.**

Artistic **Alphabets**

I won't delve too deep into this very big subject, but here are some simple ways to draw decorative letters...

 Find a font you like and copy it freehand. This L, for example, is the Holtzschue font...

1 **2** **3**

You can use the basic outline and embellish with your own touches...

1 **2** **3**

Here I got inspiration by looking up "ornate engravings" on the internet.

4

5

Draw a simple bubble or block letter and fill it in with patterns or textures.

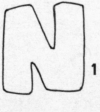 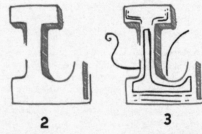

1 **2**

3 **4**

Draw a simple block letter and embellish around the outside.
Here's a 3-D letter that could use some decoration...

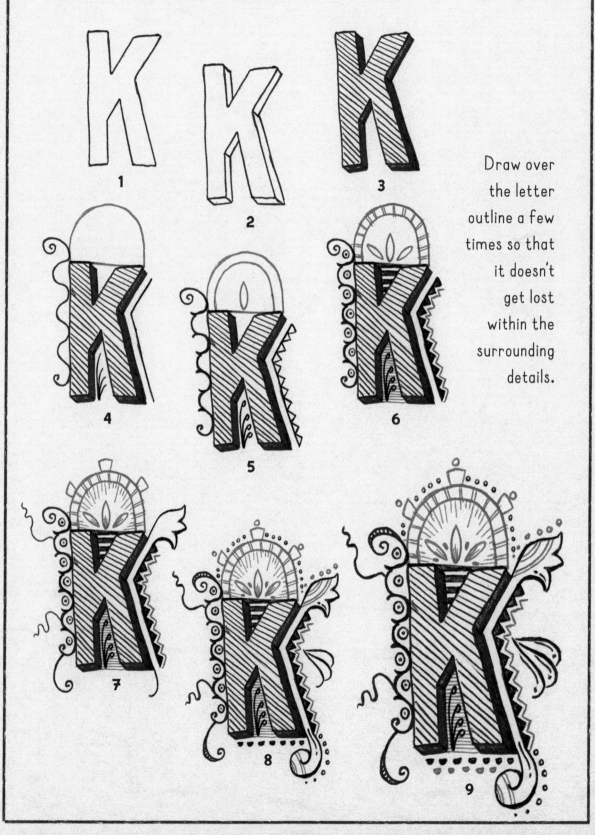

Draw over the letter outline a few times so that it doesn't get lost within the surrounding details.

MAKE A LETTER OUT OF AN OBJECT...

Remember to make sure you don't lose sight of the original letter shape altogether. It needs to be recognizable.

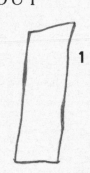  

Start simple...

...And a little more complex

Draw a letter on an object:

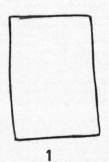  

1   2   3

4   5   6

Add a simple theme to the whole alphabet. For example, spaghetti writing:

Draw any loops
or spirals larger
than you think
they should be.
You don't want
them to get lost,
when you thicken
the letter's width.

Draw second outline
parallel to first and fill in

Make any ends rounded

Try and keep roughly the same width all
the way round, for that spaghetti look.

Add highlights while filling in:

Draw the outline of
the highlight and color
around it. Make sure
the highlight outline is
wide enough that it doesn't disappear when you fill the surrounding area!

Outline your letter
and add a drop shadow...

...Or embellish in a
contrasting color.

TIPS TO MAKE DRAWING **IN BALLPOINT** LESS TRICKY!

- Draw at a comfortable scale/size. If you are going to include a lot of detail, you don't want to be drawing on a minute scale, especially in ballpoint—it is not that fine a line! Choose a size of paper you think you can fill—for example a flower will probably require a smaller size than a cityscape.

- Drawing at an angle that is comfortable will help with accuracy. Be aware of the position of the paper in relation to where your hand/arm is resting. For example, drawing a straight line, in whatever direction you want it, is easier to achieve if you move in one fluid movement from the top to the bottom of the page. It is harder if you try to draw in a sideways direction. When drawing a circle without a stencil or compass, try rotating the paper around in a circle as you draw. With your hand resting on the page, your pen naturally moves in a curved motion.

- Ink clumps can be a pain! As you are drawing the ink heats up (due to the friction between ball and paper) and collects in tiny clumps around the ball, which then may deposit themselves onto your page. They can smudge and make your drawing look messy. Have an old piece of paper on hand to scribble on, wiping off the clumps, before you go back to your drawing, or place a plain piece of paper under your moving wrist/hand while drawing to protect the ink on the page from smudging. You can also alternate between two pens of the same color to allow them time to cool.

- Sometimes less is more: don't get bogged down with including every little detail. Leave areas blank (especially areas you feel are less important to what you are trying to portray), or you can make subtle marks with your pen to imply detail, e.g. dots instead of windows on a skyscraper. Fill in the important parts and step back from your drawing. Do you need more detail? Overcomplicating a drawing is the curse of many an artist.

- The red ballpoint is your friend! Red ink is great for drawing a faint initial outline, on top of which you can draw in the darker shades of blue and black. Red is also nice and bright, and it can really make your picture pop, contrasting with blue and/or black.

- Going over the outline of a drawn object a couple of times to thicken it looks great in pen. If your object has lot of detail within it, e.g. a texture/pattern, a strong outline helps give definition and form. Try to use the same line weight throughout the drawing, and then draw over the outline approximately two more times, or as needed, to thicken it.

- Think about the pressure you apply in your mark-making. The harder a pen is pressed to the paper, the thicker the ink will flow. Ballpoints are very sensitive to pressure and this means they can create gradient, like a pencil.

- Not sure if you can draw a certain object the way you want? Practice a few times on a scrap of paper first.

Smudging exaggerated for dramatic purposes!

TEMPLATES...

When scribbling this pen-only book, I found that the trickiest element was to get the outline just how I wanted it. With practice it becomes second nature, but until you get there, here are some of the more difficult outlines (sometimes the most simple!). You can draw on them directly, cut them out, photocopy, or trace them.

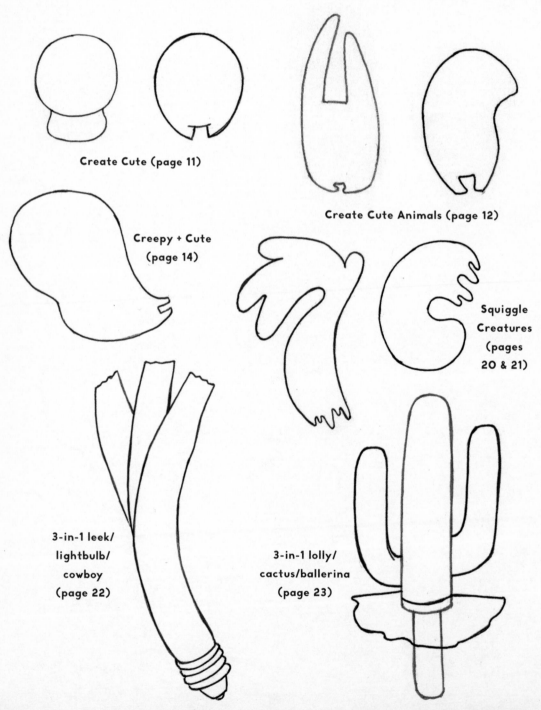

Create Cute (page 11)

Create Cute Animals (page 12)

Creepy + Cute (page 14)

Squiggle Creatures (pages 20 & 21)

3-in-1 leek/ lightbulb/ cowboy (page 22)

3-in-1 lolly/ cactus/ballerina (page 23)

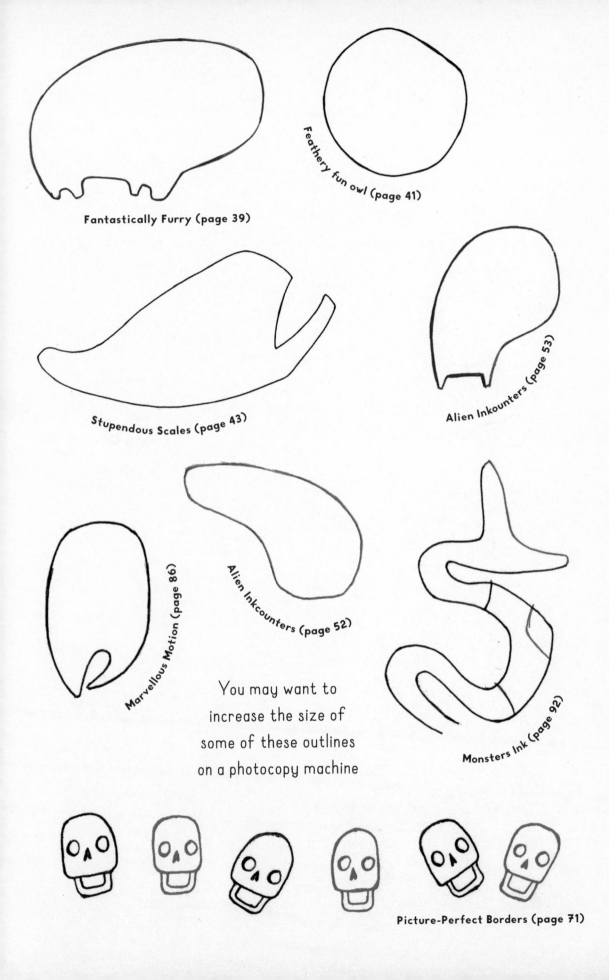

Fantastically Furry (page 39)

Feathery fun owl (page 41)

Stupendous Scales (page 43)

Alien Inkounters (page 53)

Marvellous Motion (page 86)

Alien Inkcounters (page 52)

Monsters Ink (page 92)

You may want to increase the size of some of these outlines on a photocopy machine

Picture-Perfect Borders (page 71)

Cut out...

...and fill in!

THIS LOT NEED SOME HELP IN THE HAIR DEPARTMENT!

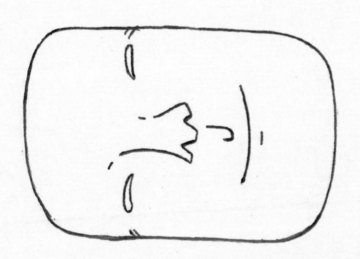

Batty Beards (page 50)

Batty Beards (page 51)

Hair Here (pages 44–46)

Hair Here (pages 44–46)

Acknowledgments...

DEDICATED TO MY
GENTLE MAN, ANDREW

He's the dude!

Additional Images

ClipArt.com 41, 64 border, 94 - **Dover Books** 16, 17, 43, 54, 96 - **fromoldbooks.org** 8
iStockphoto.com AlterYourReality 90bl; AndyWorks 91a; boggy22 90br; ChrisGorgio 52bl; Craig McCausland 39; Darumo 10; Duncan1890 6, 51, 75, 92, 95; GelatoPlus 64l; Hulton Archive 81; IJacky 90a; itpow 85; Jacus 15; JonnyJim 27; keport 86; nicoolay 62; Peeter Viisimaa 84; RolfSt 91b; wynnter 49; yaskii 64r - **Shutterstock.com** Everett Historical 48; sharpner 60, 62